GoodFood

101 FISH & SEAFOOD DISHES

10 9 8

Published in 2006 by BBC Books,
an imprint of Ebury Publishing
A Random House Group company

Recipes © BBC Magazines 2006
Photographs © BBC Magazines 2006
Book Design © Woodlands Books 2006
All the recipes contained in this book first
appeared in BBC *Good Food* Magazine

The Random House Group Limited Reg. No.
954009

Addresses for companies within the
Random House Group can be found at
www.randomhouse.co.uk

A CIP catalogue record for this book is available
from the British Library.

The Random House Group Limited supports
The Forest Stewardship Council (FSC), the
leading international forest certification organization.
All our titles that are printed on Greenpeace
approved FSC certified paper carry the FSC logo.
Our paper procurement policy can be found at:
www.rbooks.co.uk/environment

To buy books by your favourite authors and
register for offers visit www.rbooks.co.uk

Printed and bound by Firmengruppe APPL,
aprinta druck, Wemding, Germany
Colour origination by Dot Gradations Ltd

Commissioning Editor: Sarah Reece
Project Editor: Deirdre O'Reilly
Designer: Kathryn Gammon
Production: Arlene Alexander

ISBN: 978 0 563 49315 0

GoodFood
101 FISH & SEAFOOD DISHES
TRIED-AND-TESTED RECIPES

Editor
Jeni Wright

BOOKS

Contents

Introduction 6

Starters & Snacks 10

Simple Everyday Suppers 54

Easy Entertaining 100

Healthy & Low-fat   132

Storecupboard Dishes   164

Asian Flavours   188

Index   212

Introduction

Fish is good for us, and at BBC *Good Food* magazine we try to eat it regularly as part of a balanced and healthy diet. All fish contains protein, minerals and vitamins, but oily fish like herrings, sardines, salmon and mackerel are an excellent source of omega-3 fatty acids, which some nutritionists suggest keep cholesterol levels low.

With this collection of over a hundred recipes in one volume, it couldn't be easier to choose a different fish a couple of times a week, and it doesn't even have to be fresh – canned, smoked and frozen fish count just as well in the nutrition stakes. We've even put together a special chapter for fish from the cupboard, fridge and freezer, so all you need to do is add a few fresh ingredients and you'll have a nutritious meal in minutes.

Health is important, and you'll find a chapter devoted to the healthiest recipes we can find, but what most of us want these days is speed and ease as well, which is where fish really comes into its own as in the *Baked Sea Bass with Lemongrass* pictured opposite (see page 190 for the recipe). We've tested every recipe in this book in the *Good Food* kitchen, and found fish to be the ultimate convenience food: it takes hardly any cooking to be beautifully moist and tender, and the simpler the recipe the better. What higher recommendation could there be than that?

Jeni Wright
BBC *Good Food* magazine

Conversion tables

NOTES ON THE RECIPES
- Eggs are medium in the UK and Australia (large in America) unless stated otherwise.
- Wash all fresh produce before preparation.

OVEN TEMPERATURES

Gas	°C	Fan °C	°F	Oven temp.
¼	110	90	225	Very cool
½	120	100	250	Very cool
1	140	120	275	Cool or slow
2	150	130	300	Cool or slow
3	160	140	325	Warm
4	180	160	350	Moderate
5	190	170	375	Moderately hot
6	200	180	400	Fairly hot
7	220	200	425	Hot
8	230	210	450	Very hot
9	240	220	475	Very hot

APPROXIMATE WEIGHT CONVERSIONS
- All the recipes in this book list both imperial and metric measurements. Conversions are approximate and have been rounded up or down. Follow one set of measurements only; do not mix the two.
- Cup measurements, which are used by cooks in Australia and America, have not been listed here as they vary from ingredient to ingredient. Please use kitchen scales to measure dry/solid ingredients.

SPOON MEASURES

• Spoon measurements are level unless otherwise specified.

• 1 teaspoon = 5ml

• 1 tablespoon = 15ml

• 1 Australian tablespoon = 20ml (cooks in Australia should measure 3 teaspoons where 1 tablespoon is specified in a recipe)

APPROXIMATE LIQUID CONVERSIONS

metric	imperial	AUS	US
50ml	2fl oz	¼ cup	¼ cup
125ml	4fl oz	½ cup	½ cup
175ml	6fl oz	¾ cup	¾ cup
225ml	8fl oz	1 cup	1 cup
300ml	10fl oz/½ pint	½ pint	1¼ cups
450ml	16fl oz	2 cups	2 cups/1 pint
600ml	20fl oz/1 pint	1 pint	2½ cups
1 litre	35fl oz/1¾ pints	1¾ pints	1 quart

This unusual no-cook starter with its dazzling colours comes from an ancient way of preserving salmon.

Beetroot-cured Gravadlax

200g/8oz caster sugar
140g/5oz sea salt flakes
85g/3oz fresh horseradish, peeled and finely grated, or grated horseradish from a jar
3 raw beetroot (about 250g/9oz in total), coarsely grated (no need to peel)
1 bunch of fresh dill, chopped
2 salmon fillets (about 1.3kg/3lb in total), skin on and pinbones removed
salad leaves, to serve

FOR THE DRESSING
200ml carton crème fraîche
juice of 1 lemon
2 tbsp freshly grated horseradish
handful of fresh dill fronds, chopped

Takes 30 minutes, plus marinating •
Serves 8

1 In a bowl, mix the sugar, salt, horseradish, beetroot and dill to make the cure.
2 Stretch 2 large sheets of cling film over a flat surface and spoon over some of the cure. Lay 1 salmon fillet skin-side down, on the cure, then pack over most of the cure, and sandwich with the remaining fillet, skin-side up. Top with the last of the cure and wrap both fillets together tightly with lots of cling film. Place in a large roasting tray, put a smaller tray on top, weigh it down and leave in the fridge for at least 2 days (or up to 1 week). Once a day, pour away the liquid, turn the salmon over and re-apply the weights.
3 Unwrap the salmon, brush off the marinade and slice into slivers. Mix all the dressing ingredients together, season and drizzle over the salmon before serving.

• Per serving 380 kcalories, protein 30g, carbohydrate 7g, fat 26g, saturated fat 9.7g, fibre 0.5g, added sugar 5.3g, salt 3.44g

Serve in one dish for everyone to help themselves.
It's delicious with buttermilk scones.

Potted Fresh and Smoked Salmon

600g/1lb 5oz skinless salmon fillets
100g/4oz butter
200g/8oz smoked salmon
juice of 2 lemons
½ tsp chilli paste or harissa paste

Takes 20–30 minutes, plus chilling • Serves 6–8

1 Put the salmon in one layer in a microwave dish and dot with 25g/1oz of the butter and some salt and pepper. Cover with cling film and pierce several times, then microwave on High for 5–6 minutes, until the salmon is just cooked. Leave to cool.

2 Flake the salmon into a food processor, adding the juices from the dish. Chop the smoked salmon roughly and add to the processor with the lemon juice, chilli or harissa paste and some salt and pepper.

3 Process until finely chopped, but with some texture, then turn into a 1 litre/1¾ pint serving dish. Melt the remaining butter in a pan, then remove from the heat and allow the sediment to settle. Carefully pour the butter over the salmon, leaving the sediment behind. Leave to cool, then chill until set (about 2 hours).

• Per serving for six 352 kcalories, protein 29g, carbohydrate none, fat 26g, saturated fat 12g, fibre none, added sugar none, salt 2.28g

This classic salad with an Asian twist is a case of clever ingredients, with little handling, producing big results.

Spinach, Avocado and Prawn Salad

1 fresh chilli
1 garlic clove, finely chopped
finely grated zest and juice of 1 lime
1 tbsp soy sauce
1 tbsp sesame oil
200g/8oz large peeled cooked prawns
140g/5oz young spinach leaves, washed and dried
2 avocados

Takes 15–20 minutes • Serves 4

1 Finely chop the chilli, removing the seeds if you don't like too much heat. Mix in a large bowl with the garlic, lime zest and juice, soy sauce and sesame oil, then tip in the prawns and toss to coat. Cover and leave to marinate in the fridge for up to 1 hour.
2 Lift the prawns out of the marinade with a slotted spoon and set aside. Toss the spinach in the marinade until coated, then tip into a serving dish. Halve, stone and peel the avocados, then slice the flesh and tuck pieces in amongst the spinach with the prawns.

• Per serving 201 kcalories, protein 14g, carbohydrate 2g, fat 15g, saturated fat 2g, fibre 3g, added sugar 1g, salt 2.83g

You'll enjoy this indulgent snack for one so much,
you'll want to eat it every day.

Smoked Salmon and Egg Bagel

1 bagel, cut in half
1 large slice of smoked salmon
1 tbsp mayonnaise
1 tsp creamed horseradish
1 tbsp vegetable oil
1 egg
1 garlic clove, thinly sliced

Takes 10–15 minutes • Serves 1

1 Toast the cut side of one of the bagel halves. At the same time, cook the slice of salmon in a non-stick frying pan for a few seconds on each side until it turns opaque.
2 Mix the mayonnaise and horseradish together and spread over the toasted side of the bagel. Top with the salmon.
3 Heat the oil in the frying pan and fry the egg until nearly set. Toss in the garlic and let it sizzle briefly. Top the salmon with the egg, then sprinkle with the garlic slivers and black pepper to taste.

• Per serving 418 kcalories, protein 23g, carbohydrate 29g, fat 24g, saturated fat 5g, fibre 2g, added sugar none, salt 3.65g

A Spanish-style dish that's the perfect starter
when you're entertaining.

Prawns with Romesco Sauce

1 red pepper, halved lengthways
and seeded
3 fat garlic cloves, unpeeled
1 fat fresh red chilli
1 large ripe tomato
10 shelled hazelnuts
10 blanched almonds
3 sprigs of fresh parsley
120ml/4fl oz olive oil
1 small slice of day-old bread, torn
2 tbsp red wine vinegar
400g/14oz large cooked peeled tiger
prawns, defrosted and patted dry
if frozen

Takes 35–40 minutes • Serves 4–6

1 Put the pepper halves, skin-side up, in a foil-lined grill pan with the garlic, chilli and tomato. Grill for 4 minutes, turning the tomato halfway. Remove the tomato and continue grilling the pepper, garlic and chilli for 4–5 minutes until the pepper and chilli skins blacken and the garlic softens. Remove from the pan, then toast the nuts under the grill.
2 Peel, quarter and seed the tomato; peel, halve, seed and chop the chilli; peel and chop the pepper. Finely chop the nuts and parsley in a food processor; tip into a bowl.
3 Fry the pepper, garlic and chilli in 3 table-spoons of the oil for 3 minutes. Add the bread, fry until lightly browned, then chop in the food processor with the tomato, vinegar, remaining oil and some salt. Mix with the nuts and parsley, chill, then serve with the prawns.

• Per serving for four 430 kcalories, protein 26g, carbohydrate 8g, fat 33g, saturated fat 4.4g, fibre 1.8g, added sugar none, salt 2.13g

Gravadlax is a ready-to-serve gourmet treat,
making this dish a clever dinner-party cheat.

Gravadlax with Cucumber and Rye

½ cucumber, cut lengthways,
seeded and thinly sliced
3 shallots, thinly sliced
2 tbsp rice wine vinegar or cider
vinegar
2 tbsp golden caster sugar
1 tbsp roughly chopped fresh dill
2 × 140g packets gravadlax
(sold with sachets of dill and
mustard sauce)
6 slices of buttered German-style
rye bread, cut into
narrow soldiers

Takes 30 minutes • Serves 4

1 Tip the vegetables into a bowl with the vinegar, sugar and dill. Stir well and chill for up to 30 minutes.
2 On a large platter, lay out slices of scrunched-up gravadlax, then pile the vegetable salad next to it with the bread and a small bowl of the dill and mustard sauce.

• Per serving 337 kcalories, protein 13.2g, carbohydrate 38.8g, fat 16g, saturated fat 5g, fibre 3.5g, added sugar 12.1g, salt 2.57g

If you're a pesto fan, make twice as much and keep half in a jar in the fridge to stir through pasta or drizzle over roasted tomatoes.

Scallops with Rocket Pesto

handful of fresh basil
250g pack baby plum tomatoes, quartered
6 tbsp extra-virgin olive oil
18 scallops
6 slices of ciabatta or French bread
2 garlic cloves, peeled

FOR THE ROCKET PESTO
100g/4oz rocket, finely chopped
½ garlic clove, finely chopped
6 tbsp extra-virgin olive oil
4 tsp white wine vinegar

Takes 20–25 minutes • Serves 6

1 Make the rocket pesto. Mix the rocket and garlic in a large bowl with the olive oil, vinegar and some seasoning. Set aside.
2 Roughly chop the basil and put in a bowl with the tomatoes. Add 4 tablespoons of the olive oil, season and mix well.
3 Dip the scallops in the remaining 2 tablespoons of olive oil, season, then cook on a griddle or in a heavy frying pan over a high heat for 1½ minutes on each side. Toast the bread on both sides.
4 Divide the rocket pesto between six plates, and sit 3 scallops on top of each. Rub the toasted bread with the peeled garlic cloves. Put next to the scallops and spoon over some tomatoes. Serve immediately.

• Per serving 397 kcalories, protein 27g, carbohydrate 18g, fat 25g, saturated fat 3.4g, fibre 1.5g, added sugar none, salt 1.1g

Borlotti – brown beans from Italy – are very similar to cannellini, with the same oval shape and creamy texture.

Prawn and Borlotti Bean Salad

400g can borlotti beans, drained and rinsed
1 ball mozzarella cheese, drained and cut into chunks
200g/8oz cooked king prawns, peeled
1 small red onion, thinly sliced into half moons
225g pack cherry tomatoes, halved
100g bag rocket

FOR THE DRESSING
1 anchovy fillet, rinsed and finely chopped
10 capers, rinsed and chopped
1 garlic clove, finely chopped
2 tbsp red wine vinegar
6 tbsp extra-virgin olive oil

Takes 10–15 minutes • Serves 6

1 Put the beans, mozzarella, prawns, onion and tomatoes into a bowl.
2 Put the dressing ingredients in a small jar, shake well to mix, then pour over the salad and toss gently. Just before serving, toss the rocket leaves through.

• Per serving 294 kcalories, protein 19g, carbohydrate 9g, fat 20g, saturated fat 7g, fibre 3g, added sugar none, salt 2.1g

For a delicious sandwich filling for weekday lunches,
double the tuna mix.

Cheese and Paprika Tuna Melts

200g can tuna
½ bunch of spring onions, finely
chopped
4 tbsp mayonnaise
3 thick slices of granary or
wholemeal bread
50g/2oz Cheddar cheese,
coarsely grated
generous pinch of paprika

Takes 10 minutes • Serves 2

1 Preheat the grill to high. Drain the tuna,
flake it into a bowl and mix with the spring
onions and mayonnaise. Season with salt
and plenty of freshly ground black pepper.
2 Toast the bread under the grill until it's
nicely browned on both sides, then spread
the tuna mixture on top, right up to the
edges of the toast. Scatter over the cheese
and put back under the grill until the cheese
is bubbling.
3 Slice in half, sprinkle with paprika and
tuck in.

• Per serving (tuna in oil) 613 kcalories, protein 35g,
carbohydrate 29g, fat 40g, saturated fat 11g, added
sugar none, salt 2.25g

If you can't find large prawns, which look really dramatic on top of each tart, buy double the number of smaller ones.

Prawn and Asparagus Puffs

6 large fresh raw king prawns, peeled with tails left on
12–18 asparagus tips (2 or 3 per tart, your choice)
3 tbsp olive oil
300g/10oz shallots, peeled and quartered
375g pack ready-rolled puff pastry
splash of balsamic vinegar
50g pack rocket, preferably wild

FOR THE MARINADE AND DRESSING
6 tbsp olive oil
1 garlic clove, finely chopped
finely grated zest of 1 lemon
1 heaped tbsp chopped fresh parsley
1 tbsp lemon juice

Takes 30–40 minutes • Serves 6

1 Preheat the oven to 220°C/Gas 7/fan oven 200°C. For the marinade, mix the oil, garlic, lemon zest and parsley, then season. Marinate the prawns and asparagus in half the mixture, and stir the lemon juice into the remainder for the dressing.
2 Heat the oil in a pan, add the shallots, season and fry over a medium heat for 10 minutes until softened. Cut out six 10cm/4in circles from the pastry, and lay them on a baking sheet. Using a knife, mark a circle part-way through the pastry, 1cm/2in in from the edge. Bake for 10 minutes until golden.
3 Meanwhile, heat a pan, add the prawns and asparagus, and cook over a high heat for 3–4 minutes. Stir in the vinegar, take off the heat and add the rocket. Spoon the mixture and dressing onto the pastry rounds.

• Per serving 433 kcalories, protein 12g, carbohydrate 26g, fat 32g, saturated fat 8g, fibre 2g, added sugar none, salt 0.67g

The pitta breads become crunchy in the oven making them unbelievably moreish.

Smoked Salmon and Bean Dip

410g can cannellini beans, drained
and rinsed
200g carton Greek yogurt
225g pack smoked salmon
trimmings
1 tbsp chopped fresh dill
1 tbsp lemon juice

FOR THE PITTAS
6 pitta breads
2 tbsp olive oil
sea salt flakes
2 tbsp chopped fresh dill

Takes 20–30 minutes • Serves 8

1 Blend the beans and yogurt in a food processor until smooth. Add the salmon and pulse, keeping the salmon quite chunky. Tip into a bowl and stir in the dill, lemon juice and seasoning to taste. Chill until serving time.
2 For the pittas, preheat the oven to 200°C/Gas 6/fan oven 180°C. Tear the pittas onto two baking trays. Sprinkle with the oil, salt and dill. Bake for 7 minutes until crisp. Put the bowl of dip on a platter and surround with the pittas (they are equally good warm or cold).

• Per serving 526 kcalories, protein 7g, carbohydrate 69g, fat 27g, saturated fat 14g, fibre 2g, added sugar 20g, salt 0.17g

Canned tuna is a good low-fat source of protein. Remember that tuna canned in spring water contains half the calories of tuna in oil.

Tuna and Red Onion Salad

250g/9oz Charlotte potatoes
1 red onion, sliced
1 tbsp capers, rinsed and drained
200g can tuna in spring water, drained and roughly flaked
good handful of rocket or watercress

FOR THE DRESSING
4 tbsp olive oil
1 tbsp lemon juice
1 tsp Dijon mustard

Takes 30–35 minutes • Serves 2

1 Cook the potatoes in boiling salted water for 15–20 minutes or until tender. Meanwhile, make the dressing in a large bowl by whisking all the ingredients together with salt and pepper to taste.
2 Drain the potatoes and leave until cool enough to handle, then slice into chunks, leaving the skins on. Toss in the dressing with the red onion and capers, then carefully fold in the tuna and salad leaves.

• Per serving 386 kcalories, protein 20g, carbohydrate 25g, fat 23g, saturated fat 3.2g, fibre 2.5g, added sugar none, salt 1.23g

The ultimate speedy snack and so simple
that kids can make their own.

Fish Finger Torpedoes

300g pack fish fingers
1 baguette (French stick)
4–5 generous tbsp mayonnaise
5 lettuce leaves, such as cos, halved
lengthways
1 large shallot or 1 small ordinary or
red onion, thinly sliced
1 dill cucumber or 4 gherkins, thinly
sliced on the diagonal

Takes 20–30 minutes • Serves 4

1 Preheat the grill to High. Arrange the fish fingers on the grill rack and grill for 15 minutes, turning them at least once until the batter coating is crispy.
2 Slice the baguette in half down its length and ease the cut open to reveal the soft bread inside. Spread the bread generously with the mayonnaise then fill with the lettuce, shallot or onion and dill cucumber or gherkin.
3 When the fish fingers are ready, pack them into the baguette and cut across into four portions.

• Per serving 474 kcalories, protein 17g, carbohydrate 53g, fat 23g, saturated fat 3g, fibre 2g, added sugar 20g, salt 2.22g

Enjoy these fragrant and juicy
prawns with friends.

Bay-scented Prawns

2 × 20g packs of fresh basil leaves
6 tbsp olive oil
250ml jar mayonnaise
juice of 1 lime
(reserve the lime halves)
32 large fresh raw prawns, heads
and shells removed
24 small fresh bay leaves

Takes 20–30 minutes • Serves 8

1 If using wooden or bamboo skewers, soak eight in cold water for about half an hour. Plunge the basil leaves into a small pan of boiling water for about 1 minute, remove with a slotted spoon and put into a bowl of cold water.
2 Drain and squeeze out any excess water from the leaves and put into a food processor with 2 tablespoons of the olive oil. Whizz for 1–2 minutes until you have a fine paste. Add the mayonnaise and a squeeze of lime juice. Blend until smooth, transfer to a bowl and chill.
3 Thread 4 prawns and 3 bay leaves onto each skewer. Brush with the remaining oil and season well. Barbecue or grill the kebabs for 4–5 minutes, turning once, until the prawns are pink and tender. Spoon the basil mayo into the squeezed-out lime halves and serve.

• Per serving 301 kcalories, protein 11g, carbohydrate 1g, fat 28g, saturated fat 4g, fibre none, added sugar none, salt 0.65g

With just five ingredients you can create a stylish
and delicious dinner-party starter.

Smoked Salmon and Dill Tartlets

500g pack shortcrust pastry, thawed
if frozen
200g/8oz smoked salmon (or
trimmings)
2 eggs
2 tbsp chopped fresh dill, plus
a few sprigs
284ml carton single cream
lime wedges, to serve

Takes about 1 hour • Makes 6

1 Preheat the oven to 200°C/Gas 6/fan
oven 180°C. Cut the pastry into 6 pieces.
Roll out to line six 10cm/4in shallow tart tins.
Line each with a circle of greaseproof paper
and a layer of baking beans.
2 Set the cases on a baking sheet. Bake
for 10 minutes, then take from the oven,
remove the paper and beans and return to
the oven until golden (5 minutes). Reduce
the oven temperature to 180°C/Gas 4/fan
oven 160°C.
3 Cut the salmon into strips and divide
between the tartlets. Whisk the eggs and dill.
Whisk in the cream, season, and pour into
the tartlets. Bake for 15 minutes, until the
filling has set and the tops are pale gold.
Serve warm, with lime wedges and dill sprigs.

• Per serving 538 kcalories, protein 16g, carbohydrate
39g, fat 36g, saturated fat 16g, fibre 2g, added sugar
none, salt 2.06g

Tuna in olive oil gives a good kick to
this summery version of beans on toast.

Tuna-bean Toasts

12 thin slices of French bread
(depending on how many you
want to make in one go)
410g can cannellini beans, drained
and rinsed
150g can tuna in olive oil, drained
and oil reserved
handful of fresh parsley leaves,
roughly chopped
2 tomatoes, sliced
1 small red onion, finely sliced
olive oil for drizzling

Takes 10 minutes • Makes 12 slices

1 Toast the bread. Meanwhile, lightly mash
the beans. Pour 2 tablespoons of the tuna oil
over the beans, then flake in the tuna. Gently
mix in the parsley and season to taste.
2 When the toast is ready, drizzle with a little
of the tuna oil. Top the toast with a slice of
tomato and top the tomato with a spoonful
of bean mix. Scatter over the sliced onion.
Drizzle the toast with a little more oil (use
olive oil if you run out of tuna oil) and serve.

• Per serving 109 kcalories, protein 6g, carbohydrate
13g, fat 4g, saturated fat 1g, fibre 2g, added sugar
none, salt 0.52g

This is an impressive dinner-party starter
to wow your friends.

Mussels with Garlic and Cider Sauce

1.3kg/3lb mussels
85g/3oz butter
1 large garlic clove, finely chopped
1 bouquet garni
6 tbsp dry cider or white wine
handful of chopped fresh flatleaf
parsley, to finish

Takes 30 minutes • Serves 2

1 Scrub the mussels clean under the cold tap, scraping off the beards and any barnacles with a small sharp knife. Discard any mussels that are open or that do not close when tapped sharply on the work surface.
2 Melt 50g/2oz of the butter in a large pan and sizzle the garlic for 1–2 minutes. Tip in the mussels, tuck in the bouquet garni and splash in the cider or wine. Cover the pan and cook over a high heat for 4 minutes, shaking the pan occasionally, until all the mussels have opened.
3 Remove the mussels from the pan with a slotted spoon and divide between two deep bowls, discarding the bouquet garni and picking out any mussels that have not opened. Add the remaining butter to the juices in the pan and boil to reduce slightly, then stir in the parsley and pour over the mussels.

• Per serving 493 kcalories, protein 26g, carbohydrate 7g, fat 39g, saturated fat 22.7g, fibre 0.4g, added sugar none, salt 2.21g

The combined textures of the crisp toast, the meaty prawns, the creamy eggs and the sweet tomatoes make this a satisfying speedy snack.

Prawn Piperade

4 eggs
2 tbsp milk
1 tbsp olive oil
2 handfuls of large cooked prawns
(about 175g/6oz), defrosted and
patted dry if frozen
8 cherry tomatoes, halved

TO SERVE
buttered toast
small handful of fresh flatleaf
parsley, chopped

Takes 10–15 minutes • Serves 2

1 Beat the eggs with the milk and a pinch each of salt and pepper. Set aside.
2 Heat the oil in a medium frying pan, tip in the prawns and tomatoes and fry over a high heat just until the tomatoes start to burst. By now everything should be nice and hot.
3 Pour the beaten eggs into the pan and let them sit for 20 seconds. Fold over the eggs from the bottom of the pan with a wooden spoon, let them sit again, then stir once more. (This way of cooking the eggs stops them from getting over-scrambled.) When softly set, spoon the mixture over hot buttered toast, scatter with parsley and serve.

• Per serving 298 kcalories, protein 33g, carbohydrate 2g, fat 18g, saturated fat 4g, fibre none, added sugar none, salt 3.92g

Fresh crab is pricey but for a special occasion
it's worth splashing out.

Spicy Potted Crab

2 × 250g packs unsalted butter
½–¾ tsp hot chilli powder, to taste
350g/12oz fresh (well picked over) or
frozen (defrosted) white crabmeat
2 tbsp finely chopped fresh chives
2 tbsp finely chopped fresh flatleaf
parsley
finely grated zest and juice of
1 small lemon
small pinch of freshly grated nutmeg
lemon wedges and Melba toast,
to serve

Takes about 1 hour, plus chilling •
Serves 6–8

1 Melt the butter in a pan. Increase the heat a little to separate most of the milk solids, but don't let the butter burn. When there are nutty brown bits at the bottom and the remaining liquid is clear, cool slightly and pour into a jug, leaving the nutty bits behind. Pour the clear butter back into a clean pan and tip in the chilli powder. Heat gently for 1–2 minutes.
2 Put the rest of the ingredients in a bowl and season. Carefully fold together, adjust seasoning, then spoon into 6–8 ramekins.
3 Pour over the clarified butter to give a thin covering (stirring the butter before you pour). If the butter cools, microwave it for half a minute. Cover the ramekins, chill for 2 hours.
4 Remove the potted crab from the fridge an hour before serving, but keep in a cool place. Serve with lemon wedges and Melba toast.

• Per serving for six 665 kcalories, protein 11g, carbohydrate none, fat 69g, saturated fat 43.4g, fibre 0.1g, added sugar none, salt 0.84g

This is an elegant low-fat dish that's perfect
as a starter or a lunchtime snack.

Smoked Salmon with Pea Pancakes

85g/3oz plain flour
1 egg
100ml/3½fl oz milk
200g/8oz fresh or frozen peas
vegetable oil, for frying

FOR THE DIP
6 tbsp fromage frais
1 tbsp creamed horseradish

TO SERVE
200g/8oz smoked salmon
fresh chives, snipped

Takes 25–30 minutes • Serves 4

1 Make the dip: mix together the fromage frais and creamed horseradish and set aside.
2 Make a batter with the flour, egg and milk. Season. Steam the peas for about 5 minutes if fresh or 2 minutes if frozen, and put into a bowl. Using a potato masher, crush the peas until roughly mashed and add to the pancake batter.
3 Heat a drop of oil in a frying pan until smoking. Turn the heat down and add 3 separate tablespoons of batter. When small holes appear on the tops of the pancakes, flip them over and cook the other sides for about 30 seconds. Keep warm. Cook the remaining batter in the same way.
4 Put 3 pancakes on each plate and top with smoked salmon and chives. Serve with the dip on the side.

• Per serving 281 kcalories, protein 23g, carbohydrate 26g, fat 10g, saturated fat 3g, fibre 3g, added sugar none, salt 2.59g

Make this dish your own by adding flaked canned tuna, sliced hard-boiled egg, roasted peppers or thinly sliced onion – perfect picnic food.

Anchovy Pan Bagnat

1 country-style loaf or large baguette
4 tbsp olive oil
1 tbsp white wine vinegar
2 garlic cloves, chopped
500g/1lb 2oz ripe vine tomatoes
1 tbsp capers
2–3 tbsp chopped stoned black olives
8–10 anchovy fillets
handful of fresh basil leaves

Takes 20 minutes, plus soaking time • Cuts into 8 slices

1 Split the loaf in half lengthways. Drizzle both cut surfaces with olive oil and scatter the vinegar and garlic on the bottom half. Sprinkle both cut sides with salt and pepper.
2 Roughly chop the tomatoes and spread over the bottom half, then sprinkle over the capers and olives. Lay the anchovies on top, scatter with basil leaves and press everything down lightly.
3 Cover the filling with the other half of the loaf and press down firmly. Wrap tightly in foil or cling film and place a weight on top for at least half an hour, longer if you have the time (4 hours maximum). Unwrap and cut into thick slices.

• Per serving 246 kcalories, protein 8g, carbohydrate 38g, fat 8g, saturated fat 1g, fibre 3g, added sugar none, salt 1.47g

These rösti are also good made with
a drained can of tuna instead.

Prawn and Corn Rösti

1kg/2lb 4oz floury potatoes, such as
Maris Piper or King Edward
175g/6oz frozen sweetcorn
1 bunch of spring onions, finely
chopped
200g/8oz peeled prawns, defrosted
and patted dry if frozen,
roughly chopped
large handful of fresh parsley,
chopped
generous knob of butter
good splash of vegetable oil

Takes 50 minutes • Serves 4

1 Boil the potatoes in their skins for
20–25 minutes until just tender. Leave to
cool, then peel and grate coarsely into a
large bowl.
2 Boil the corn for 3 minutes, drain well and
add to the potatoes with the spring onions,
prawns, parsley and some salt and pepper.
Mix well.
3 Shape the mixture into 8 cakes, dust
lightly with flour, and chill.
4 Heat the butter and oil in a pan, add
4 potato cakes and fry for 3 minutes, flip
over and fry for a further 3–4 minutes, until
crisp and golden. Remove and keep warm
while you cook the rest of the cakes.

• Per serving 325 kcalories, protein 19g, carbohydrate
51g, fat 6g, saturated fat 2.1g, fibre 4.5g, added
sugar none, salt 1.12g

To reduce the fat content for an even healthier dish, use only half a can of coconut milk and add 200ml/7fl oz vegetable or chicken stock.

Sweet and Spicy Fish

3 tbsp medium curry paste
1 large onion, halved and sliced
1 red pepper, seeded and thickly sliced
small bunch of fresh coriander, leaves and stems separated and roughly chopped
400ml can reduced-fat coconut milk
large handful of dried mango, chopped
700g/1lb 9oz skinless firm white fish fillets, cut into large chunks
naan breads, to serve

Takes 25 minutes • Serves 4

1 Heat the curry paste in a large saucepan and fry the onion for 3 minutes until starting to soften. Stir in the sliced pepper and coriander stems and cook for another 2 minutes. Pour in the coconut milk, tip in the mango pieces and bring to the boil. Season to taste, turn down the heat and simmer for 5 minutes until slightly thickened.
2 Add the fish and cook for 3–5 minutes or until it flakes easily. Sprinkle the coriander leaves over the curry just before serving with warmed naan breads.

• Per serving 332 kcalories, protein 35g, carbohydrate 18g, fat 14g, saturated fat 9.2g, fibre 2.2g, added sugar none, salt 1g

Jazz up white fish fillets with this
amazingly tasty recipe.

Fish Cakes with Chilli Cream

650g/1lb 7oz floury potatoes, such
as Maris Piper or King Edward,
peeled
225g/8½oz shelled young broad
beans
900g/2lb firm white fish or salmon
fillets
plain flour, for dusting
olive oil, for shallow frying
crème fraîche and chilli sauce,
to serve

Takes 40–50 minutes • Serves 4

1 Cook the potatoes in boiling salted water for 20 minutes, adding the beans for the last 5 minutes. Meanwhile, poach the fish in 600ml/1 pint water in a saucepan for 8–10 minutes until tender.

2 Drain the fish and cool slightly, then flake into chunky pieces, discarding any skin and bones. Drain the potatoes and beans and mash together. Fold the fish into the mash and season, then shape into 8 patties and dust lightly with flour.

3 Cover the bottom of a non-stick frying pan with oil and heat until hot, then fry the fish cakes for 3–4 minutes on each side until golden brown. Serve with a pot of crème fraîche, drizzled with chilli sauce.

• Per serving 458 kcalories, protein 48g, carbohydrate 38g, fat 14g, saturated fat 1.9g, fibre 5.8g, added sugar none, salt 0.37g

Any white fish will work well in this
superhealthy soup.

Chunky Fish Soup

2 tsp olive oil
2 leeks, finely sliced
550g/1lb 4oz potatoes, cut into
small cubes
1 litre/1¾ pints fish stock (use
a cube)
pared zest of 1 lemon
300ml/½ pint full-fat milk
330g can sweetcorn, drained and
rinsed
250g/9oz boneless, skinless salmon,
cut into chunks
250g/9oz boneless, skinless white
fish, cut into chunks
handful of fresh chives, snipped
2 tbsp double cream (optional)

Takes 40 minutes • Serves 3–4

1 Heat the oil in a large saucepan, tip in
the leeks and fry gently for 5 minutes until
softened, but not coloured. Add the potatoes
and cook for a further minute. Pour in the
stock and lemon zest, cover and simmer
for 12–15 minutes or until the potatoes are
tender. With a slotted spoon, remove half
the potatoes and leeks from the stock and
set aside.
2 Transfer the remaining potatoes, leeks,
stock and milk to a blender or food processor
and whizz until smooth. Pour back into the
pan, and add the sweetcorn, fish and
reserved vegetables. Cover and heat gently
for 3–4 minutes until the fish is just cooked
through – don't boil. Stir in the chives, and
cream (if using), then season to taste.

• Per serving for three 567 kcalories, protein 43g,
carbohydrate 63g, fat 18g, saturated fat 4.9g, fibre
5.5g, added sugar 4.5g, salt 1.1g

A small trout is the perfect whole fish. And what's more,
it tastes just as delicious hot or cold.

Tangy Trout

1 lemon
1 small bunch of fresh dill, half
chopped, half left as sprigs
1 rainbow trout, gutted and washed,
weighing about 350g/12oz
2 tbsp olive oil, plus a little extra
for greasing
2 tbsp Greek yogurt
4 runner beans, string removed and
thinly sliced on the diagonal
3 radishes, sliced into thin rounds

Takes 25–35 minutes • Serves 1

1 Preheat the oven to 200°C/Gas 6/fan
oven 180°C. Slice half the lemon and stuff
the slices and the sprigs of dill into the cavity
of the trout. Lay the fish on an oiled baking
sheet and make 4 diagonal slashes in the
skin. Drizzle 1 tablespoon of the oil over the
fish, season and bake for 15 minutes.
2 Meanwhile, stir the chopped dill into the
yogurt with a squeeze of lemon and some
salt and pepper, and set aside.
3 Cook the runner beans in boiling salted
water for 3–4 minutes until tender but still
slightly crunchy. Drain and toss with the
radishes and remaining oil.
4 Serve the fish with the warm beans and
the yogurt sauce. Trim the remaining lemon
into a wedge to squeeze over the trout and
the salad.

• Per serving 557 kcalories, protein 46g, carbohydrate
4g, fat 39g, saturated fat 7.4g, fibre 1.5g, added sugar
none, salt 0.32g

A tasty way of getting your kids to eat fish and greens.
Any leftover filling will make a delicious lunch the following day.

Smoky Colcannon Jackets

2 large baking potatoes, each weighing about 250g/9oz
100g/4oz skinned smoked cod or haddock (undyed is best)
3 smoked back bacon rashers, snipped into pieces
5 tbsp milk
25g/1oz butter
1 Savoy cabbage, very finely shredded

Takes 40–50 minutes • Serves 2

1 Prick the potatoes with a fork, then put them on a microwave dish lined with kitchen paper. Cook on High for 6 minutes, then turn them over and cook for 7 minutes. Leave until cool enough to handle.

2 Put the fish and bacon in a large microwave bowl with the milk and butter. Cook on High for 4 minutes, then break the fish into flakes. Cook the cabbage in a pan of boiling water for 3 minutes and drain. Preheat the oven to 220°C/Gas 7/fan oven 200°C.

3 Cut a slim slice lengthways off each potato. Scoop out the flesh (keeping the potato skins whole) and add to the fish and bacon mixture. Then add the cabbage, season and mash together. Spoon the mixture back into the skins, piling it high, then bake for 15–20 minutes.

• Per serving 431 kcalories, protein 23g, carbohydrate 47g, fat 18g, saturated fat 9g, fibre 5g, added sugar none, salt 3.29g

Double the ingredients if you're
feeding a large crowd.

Tuna, Potato and Spinach Salad

500g/1lb 2oz small new potatoes
2 tbsp pesto sauce
3 tbsp olive oil
1 tbsp white wine vinegar
½ × 225g bag washed-and-ready-to-
use young leaf spinach
2 roasted red peppers from a jar,
drained and cut into strips
2 × 200g cans tuna (any kind),
drained and flaked

Takes 20–30 minutes • Serves 4

1 Bring a large pan of salted water to the boil. Add the potatoes, bring back to the boil and cook for 15–20 minutes until tender.
2 Whisk the pesto with the olive oil and vinegar and season with salt and pepper.
3 Drain the potatoes. While they are still hot, tip them into a large bowl with the spinach, peppers and dressing. Toss everything together so the heat from the potatoes gently wilts the spinach and the dressing coats all the leaves. Now add the tuna and carefully toss again to keep the tuna in fairly large flakes. Serve immediately.

• Per serving 448 kcalories, protein 27g, carbohydrate 34g, fat 24g, saturated fat 4g, fibre 4g, added sugar none, salt 2.23g

If you prefer to cook the parcels in the oven, they will take
15 minutes at 190°C/Gas 5/fan oven 170°C.

Leeky Salmon in a Parcel

2 salmon fillets, about
140g/5oz each
1 medium or 2 small leeks, about
200g/8oz in total
50g/2oz frozen petits pois
4 heaped tbsp crème fraîche, plus
2 tbsp to serve
1 tbsp chopped fresh tarragon

Takes 15–20 minutes • Serves 2

1 Season the salmon fillets all over. Slice the leeks very thinly. Cut two 40cm/16in square sheets of greaseproof paper and put a fillet in the middle of each sheet.
2 Top each fillet with leeks and peas, and 2 tablespoons of the crème fraîche. Sprinkle with tarragon and some salt and pepper.
3 Make up parcels with the paper and stand them on a microwave-plate or tray. Microwave on High for 5 minutes. Put the contents of the parcels on two plates and top each serving with a spoonful of crème fraîche.

• Per serving 535 kcalories, protein 34g, carbohydrate 8g, fat 41g, saturated fat 19g, fibre 3g, added sugar none, salt 0.41g

You can use any fillets of white fish for this grown-up food for kids. For a lighter meal, serve the goujons with dips instead of the vegetables.

Sole Goujons

4 lemon sole fillets (from 2 whole fish), about 500g/1lb 2oz in total
2 large eggs
113g pack natural breadcrumbs
olive oil, for frying

Takes 50–60 minutes, including chilling • Serves 2–3

1 Trim the side flaps off the fish and cut each fillet in half lengthways, then cut across into bite-size pieces.

2 Beat the eggs with a fork in a large bowl. Tip the breadcrumbs into a large shallow dish, and mix in some salt and pepper.

3 Dip the pieces of fish in the eggs, then coat in the breadcrumbs. Chill in the fridge for 30 minutes.

4 Heat 3 tablespoons olive oil in a non-stick frying pan over a high heat until hot. Add a batch of goujons and cook for 2–3 minutes on each side until golden and crisp. Wipe the pan with kitchen paper and heat another 2–3 tablespoons of oil between batches.

• Per serving 363 kcalories, protein 18.9g, carbohydrate 15g, fat 25.8g, saturated fat 4.2g, fibre none, added sugar none, salt 0.46g

A fresh take on salsa that's the ideal
accompaniment to lightly-fried fish.

Pan-fried Fish with Beetroot Salsa

4 firm white fish fillets, skin on
a little plain flour
25g/1oz butter
2 tbsp olive oil

FOR THE BEETROOT SALSA
4 small cooked beetroot, diced
8 spring onions, chopped
1 fresh red chilli, seeded and finely
chopped
2 tbsp chopped fresh mint
2 tbsp lemon juice
3 tbsp olive oil

Takes 30 minutes • Serves 4

1 Make the salsa. Put the diced beetroot in a bowl with the spring onions, chilli, mint, lemon juice and olive oil. Season and stir well.

2 Dust the fish lightly with flour. Melt the butter in a heavy frying pan with the olive oil and fry the fish for 3–4 minutes on each side until the flesh flakes easily. Serve hot, with the beetroot salsa.

• Per serving 350 kcalories, protein 34g, carbohydrate 9g, fat 20g, saturated fat 5.4g, fibre 1.2g, added sugar none, salt 0.48g

Cheer yourself up on a cold winter's night with this
simple supper dish that everyone will love.

Hot Smoked Mackerel Jackets

4 baking potatoes
2–3 tbsp horseradish sauce, or
to taste
100ml/3½fl oz skimmed milk,
warmed
1 bunch of spring onions, thinly
sliced
4 smoked mackerel fillets, skinned
and flaked

Takes 20 minutes • Serves 4

1 Cook the potatoes in the microwave on High for 10 minutes until softened, turning over halfway. Halve the potatoes lengthways and, using a spoon, scoop out the flesh into a bowl, leaving a shell of potato around the skin. Pre-heat the grill to high.

2 Mash the potato flesh with the horseradish sauce and milk until smooth and creamy, then fold in the spring onions and mackerel. Season to taste, adding more horseradish sauce if you like, then spoon the mash back into the potato skins. Place on a baking tray and grill for 5 minutes until the mash is heated through and golden on top.

• Per serving 553 kcalories, protein 28g, carbohydrate 24g, fat 39g, saturated fat 9.5g, fibre 2.1g, added sugar 0.2g, salt 2.49g

Finnan haddock is split, brined and cold-smoked. It's a traditional ingredient in this soup, but you can use undyed smoked haddock fillets.

Cullen Skink

2 Finnan haddock or 500g/1lb 2oz undyed smoked haddock fillets
2 onions, chopped
600g/1lb 5oz potatoes, peeled and finely diced (about 2 large potatoes)
450ml/16fl oz full-fat milk
25g/1oz unsalted butter
double cream and snipped fresh chives, to finish

Takes 40–45 minutes • Serves 6

1 Put the fish in a large pan with 300ml/½ pint cold water. Bring to the boil and simmer for 5–10 minutes until the fish is cooked (Finnan haddock will need a little longer than fillets). Remove, peel off the skin and flake the flesh into large chunks. Discard any bones.
2 Add the onions and potatoes to the liquid in the pan with plenty of pepper. Pour in some of the milk to cover the vegetables if needed, cover the pan and cook over a medium heat for 12–15 minutes until tender.
3 Remove from the heat. Mash the vegetables, retaining some of the texture. Add the rest of the milk and the butter and bring to the boil, then simmer for a few minutes. Add the fish and reheat gently for 2–3 minutes. Season to taste. Serve in warm bowls with cream and chives.

• Per serving 287 kcalories, protein 21g, carbohydrate 24g, fat 13g, saturated fat 7.2g, fibre 1.9g, added sugar none, salt 1.72g

Tabbouleh is a classic Middle-Eastern dish that's perfect with fish. And couscous is an excellent versatile alternative to pasta or rice.

Salmon with Tabbouleh Salad

4 skinless salmon fillets, about 175g/6oz each
120ml/4fl oz olive oil
250g/9oz couscous
4 ripe tomatoes, finely diced
½ cucumber, finely diced
1 bunch of spring onions, thinly sliced
2 × 20g packs fresh flatleaf parsley, finely chopped
finely grated zest of 1 lemon
2 tbsp lemon juice
1 garlic clove, crushed

Takes 30–35 minutes • Serves 4

1 Preheat the grill to high. Brush the salmon with 2 tablespoons of the oil and season well. Tip the couscous into a bowl, pour over 300ml/½ pint boiling water and stir, then cover with a plate and leave to stand.
2 Grill the salmon for 6 minutes, turning once. While the salmon is cooking, fluff up the couscous with a fork, then toss in the remaining oil and all the other ingredients. Add salt and pepper to taste and mix well.
3 Divide the tabbouleh salad between four plates and top with the salmon. Serve immediately.

• Per serving 731 kcalories, protein 41g, carbohydrate 37g, fat 48g, saturated fat 7.9g, fibre 2.1g, added sugar none, salt 0.24g

A tasty fish idea that will
boost your health.

Herbed Salmon Fillets

2 skinless salmon fillets, about
175g/6oz each
3 tbsp extra-virgin olive oil
grated zest and juice of 1 lemon
4 tbsp chopped fresh herbs (e.g.
parsley, chives and tarragon)
400g/14oz new potatoes, quartered
or halved
100g/4oz spring greens, shredded
1 garlic clove, crushed

Takes 30–40 minutes • Serves 2

1 Put the salmon in an ovenproof dish and coat with 1 tablespoon of the oil, the lemon zest and half of the herbs. Preheat the grill to high.

2 Cook the potatoes in boiling salted water for 8 minutes. Place the greens in a steamer on top of the potatoes, cover and continue cooking for 7–8 minutes or until the greens and potatoes are tender. Meanwhile, grill the salmon fleshy side up for 8 minutes or until the flesh flakes easily.

3 Drain the potatoes and crush roughly with the garlic and the remaining oil and herbs. Mix in the greens, then divide between two plates and top with the salmon. Pour any juices from the grill pan over the salmon and serve immediately.

• Per serving 469 kcalories, protein 23g, carbohydrate 35g, fat 27g, saturated fat 4.3g, fibre 4g, added sugar none, salt 0.19g

To make this even more healthy, use reduced-fat
mayonnaise and tuna in brine.

Hearty Tuna Salad

350g/12oz new potatoes
4 anchovy fillets
4 tbsp mayonnaise
splash white wine vinegar
or juice 1 lemon
1 large cos lettuce
bunch of spring onions, chopped
2 × 185g cans tuna steak
in brine or oil

Takes 25–30 minutes • Serves 4

1 Boil the potatoes in a saucepan for
15 minutes or until tender. Drain and cool
under cold water.
2 Meanwhile, make the dressing by mashing
the anchovy fillets with the mayonnaise.
Add the white wine vinegar or lemon juice
and season to taste with black pepper.
3 Tear the leaves from the lettuce into a
large bowl. Slice the potatoes and add to the
bowl together with the spring onions. Drain
the tuna and flake into the bowl. Drizzle the
dressing over and serve.

• Per serving 259 kcalories, protein 21g, carbohydrate
16g, fat 13g, saturated fat 2g, fibre 1.8g, added sugar
2.8g, salt 1.11g

This is a dish with a bit of zing and is
ideal for mid-week suppers.

Cod with Lemon and Parsley

2 cod fillets, about 175/6oz each
seasoned flour
1 lemon
25g/1oz butter
1 heaped tbsp chopped fresh
parsley
new potatoes and greens or runner
beans, to serve

Takes 20 minutes • Serves 2

1 Coat the cod fillets with the flour. Dust
off any excess. Squeeze the juice from
the lemon.
2 Heat half the butter in a frying pan. When
it is bubbling, add the fish and cook over a
fairly high heat until the underside is done
(about 4–5 minutes). Using a fish slice, turn
the fillets carefully and brown the other side.
When the fish is just cooked (the flesh will
start to flake and become opaque), add the
remaining butter to the pan. When it is
bubbling, stir in the lemon juice and season.
3 Bubble the sauce up until it is slightly
thickened, then stir in the parsley. Serve with
new potatoes and greens or runner beans.

• Per serving 277 kcalories, protein 34g, carbohydrate
9g, fat 12g, saturated fat 7g, fibre 1g, added sugar
none, salt 0.77g

You'll find the salmon is really succulent cooked in this way, and works well with the curry and lentils.

Spicy Salmon and Lentils

2 tsp curry paste
410g can green lentils, drained and rinsed
2 salmon fillets, about 175g/6oz each
3 tbsp olive oil
juice of 1 lemon
2 large handfuls of baby spinach

Takes 15 minutes • Serves 2

1 Heat a large, lidded shallow pan over a medium heat. Tip in the curry paste and fry briefly, stirring constantly, until sizzling and aromatic. Add the lentils with about a quarter of a can of water and season. Heat until simmering then lay the salmon on top, skin-side up. Cover and leave the salmon to cook for 6–8 minutes until it feels firm.

2 While the salmon is cooking, make the dressing. Mix together the olive oil and lemon juice and season well. When the salmon is cooked, lift it out of the pan with a fish slice and set aside.

3 Turn the heat up, stir in the spinach and a third of the dressing and cook until the spinach has just wilted. Spoon the lentils and spinach onto two plates, sit the salmon on top and drizzle over the remaining dressing.

• Per serving 600 kcalories, protein 46g, carbohydrate 20g, fat 38g, saturated fat 7g, fibre 4g, added sugar none, salt 2.35g

A delicious mid-week meal that's
both warming and nutritious.

Salmon and Potato Grill

650g/1lb 7oz new potatoes, skin on,
sliced lengthways
100g/4oz frozen peas
200g can salmon
200ml tub crème fraîche
100g/4oz mature Cheddar cheese,
coarsely grated

Takes 25 minutes • Serves 4

1 Boil the potatoes in salted water for about 10 minutes, until almost tender but not breaking up. Tip in the frozen peas and simmer for another 2–3 minutes. Drain well then tip into a mixing bowl. Preheat the grill to high.

2 Drain the salmon and flake into chunks, then gently toss with the potatoes and peas. Season to taste and spoon into a shallow flameproof dish.

3 Dollop the crème fraîche on top, roughly spread it over, and then scatter over the cheese. Grill for a few minutes until bubbling and golden.

• Per serving 465 kcalories, protein 22g, carbohydrate 31g, fat 29g, saturated fat 15g, fibre 3g, added sugar none, salt 1.10g

Steaming the haddock over the simmering potatoes and kale retains all the flavour of the fish and gives the vegetables a lovely smokiness.

Smoked Haddock with Kale Mash

1 medium potato, peeled and chopped into small chunks
200ml/7fl oz vegetable stock
large handful of kale, finely shredded
small knob of butter
140g/5oz piece skinned smoked haddock (undyed is best)
25g/1oz butter
1 heaped tbsp Dijon mustard

Takes 30–40 minutes • Serves 1

1 Boil the potato in the stock for 6 minutes until the potato fluffs round the edges and the stock has reduced slightly. Stir in the kale and butter, lower the heat and simmer, covered, for 5 minutes. Lay the haddock on top of the kale and potatoes, cover the pan and steam gently for 5 minutes.
2 Meanwhile, melt the butter in a microwave or a pan on top of the stove, then whisk in the mustard, a splash of water, a tiny pinch of salt and a good grinding of pepper.
3 Using a fish slice, lift out the cooked haddock and set aside, keeping it on the fish slice. Mash the potato and kale in the pan with the pan juices. Scoop the mash onto a plate, sit the haddock on top and pour over the sauce.

• Per serving 459 kcalories, protein 34g, carbohydrate 21g, fat 27g, saturated fat 15g, fibre 3g, added sugar none, salt 6.21g

This simple dish is bursting with lively flavours and is low fat to boot.

Herby Cod Bake

4 tbsp natural low-fat yogurt
2 tbsp sun-dried tomato pesto
2 tbsp chopped fresh parsley or dill
2 skinless cod or haddock fillets, about 175g/6oz each
salad and crusty bread, to serve

Takes 15 minutes •
Serves 2 (easily doubled)

1 Preheat the grill to high. Mix the yogurt, pesto and 1 tablespoon of the parsley or dill. Season and pour over the fish fillets in a shallow ovenproof or microwaveable dish, covering them completely.
2 Grill for 4–5 minutes without turning until the fish fillets are cooked through to the middle. Or cover the dish with cling film and microwave on High for 3 minutes.
3 Sprinkle the remaining parsley or dill over the dish and serve with salad and crusty bread.

• Per serving 247 kcalories, protein 36g, carbohydrate 3g, fat 10g, saturated fat 4g, fibre 3g, added sugar none, salt 0.53g

Yummy, creamy comfort
food at its best.

Salmon and Rocket Pasta

1 tsp oil
2 fresh salmon fillets, skin on
200g/8oz tagliatelle
100g bag rocket
2 tbsp crème fraîche
zest of ½ lemon

Takes 20 minutes •
Serves 2 (easily doubled)

1 Heat the oil in a non-stick pan and cook the salmon, skin-side down, for 5 minutes. Turn over and continue to cook for 4 minutes more until the salmon is cooked through. Remove from the pan, leave to cool, then flake the fish into large chunks, discarding the skin.

2 Cook the tagliatelle according to pack instructions. Scoop out half a cup of cooking water, then drain the pasta and return to the pan. Toss in the salmon and remaining ingredients, loosening with the cooking water if the mixture is too thick. Serve immediately.

• Per serving 682 kcalories, protein 42g, carbohydrate 77g, fat 25g, saturated fat 7g, fibre 4g, added sugar none, salt 0.21g

Herring flesh has a delicate flavour that works well
with many fresh herbs, particularly basil.

Herrings with Mustard and Basil

4 × 85g/3oz herring fillets, or
4 × 225g/8oz herrings, gutted
4 tbsp extra-virgin olive oil
2 tbsp wholegrain mustard
large bunch of fresh basil,
roughly torn
1 tsp clear honey
grated zest and juice of 1 lemon

Takes 15 minutes • Serves 4

1 Preheat the grill to high. Rinse the fish
under running cold water to dislodge any
loose scales. Brush with a little of the oil and
season lightly. Grill for 6–8 minutes, or until
cooked; the skin should be well browned
and the flesh firm and opaque.
2 Meanwhile, make the dressing. Whisk the
mustard, basil, honey, lemon zest and juice
and the remaining oil in a small bowl, and
season to taste. Once the fish is cooked,
spoon the dressing over and serve.

• Per serving 258 kcalories, protein 14g, carbohydrate
2g, fat 22g, saturated fat 3g, fibre 1g, added sugar
1g, salt 0.54g

Hoki is a New Zealand import and is available in the freezer cabinet in supermarkets. It's a firm, white-textured fish similar to cod.

Cheat's Bouillabaisse

500g carton tomato sauce for pasta
450ml/12fl oz fish stock (use a cube)
2 courgettes, finely sliced
1 bulb fennel, finely sliced
450g/1lb hoki or cod fillets,
defrosted if frozen
handful of fresh basil leaves, torn

TO SERVE
1 tsp chipotle chillies in adobo
sauce or chilli paste
5 tbsp half-fat crème fraîche

Takes 15 minutes • Serves 4

1 Bring the pasta sauce and stock to the boil in a large pan and simmer for 2–3 minutes. Add the courgettes and fennel and simmer for a further 2 minutes.
2 Cut the fish into 4cm/1½in pieces. Add to the soup and poach over a low heat for 2–3 minutes or until the fish is cooked. Do not stir, or the fish will break up. Gently stir in the basil and adjust the seasoning.
3 To serve, mix the chipotle chilli mix or chilli paste with the crème fraîche and season. Ladle the soup into bowls and spoon a dollop of crème fraîche on top.

• Per serving 164 kcalories, protein 23g, carbohydrate 9g, fat 4g, saturated fat 1g, fibre 3g, added sugar 5g, salt 1.83g

A healthy supper dish that's so delicious
you'll want to eat it again and again.

Grilled Fish with New Potato Crush

450g/1lb new potatoes
50g/2oz butter
1 bunch of spring onions, thinly
sliced
4 firm white fish fillets, skin on
1 bunch of watercress, to garnish
mayonnaise, to serve (optional)

Takes 40 minutes • Serves 4

1 Cook the potatoes in boiling salted water
for 15 minutes or until tender. Meanwhile,
preheat the grill to high. At the same time,
melt the butter in a heavy pan and soften the
spring onions for 3–4 minutes.
2 Lay the fish, skin-side up, on a
buttered tray and cook under the grill for
8–10 minutes until the skin is crisp and
the flesh flakes easily.
3 Drain the potatoes and tip into the pan
of spring onions, off the heat. Crush the
potatoes lightly and mix with the spring
onions. Season to taste. Divide the crush
between four plates, top with the fish and
garnish with watercress. Serve mayonnaise
in a separate bowl, for those who like it.

• Per serving 322 kcalories, protein 35g, carbohydrate
19g, fat 12g, saturated fat 6.8g, fibre 1.8g, added
sugar none, salt 0.52g

The sweet scallops and chestnuts are set off perfectly
well by the rich flavour of the ceps.

Scallops with Ceps and Chestnuts

85g/3oz unsalted butter
1 small onion, finely chopped
3 garlic cloves, finely chopped
8 medium ceps (about 400g/14oz),
cleaned
150ml/¼ pint dry white wine
12 cooked whole chestnuts
8 large sprigs of fresh thyme,
(2 whole and 6 with the leaves
picked from the stalks)
2 tbsp sunflower oil
12 large scallops, corals removed

Takes about 1¼ hours • Serves 4

1 Heat half the butter in a pan and sweat the onion and garlic for 5 minutes. Separate the cep stalks from the heads, cut the stalks into chunks and cut the heads in half. Set aside.
2 Stir the cep stalks into the onions, increase the heat and fry for 2 minutes. Pour in the wine and reduce by half. Add the chestnuts, 2 thyme sprigs and 400ml/14fl oz water. Bring to the boil, then simmer for 40 minutes.
3 Heat the oil in a large frying pan. Put in the cep heads, cut side down, around the outside, then put the scallops in the centre. Fry over a high heat for 1 minute on each side, turn over and fry for 2 minutes more. Sprinkle over the thyme leaves, season and turn off the heat.
4 Remove the thyme sprigs from the compôte and stir in the remaining butter. Serve in deep plates, topped with the scallops and ceps.

• Per serving 381 kcalories, protein 17g, carbohydrate 16g, fat 25g, saturated fat 12g, fibre 3g, added sugar none, salt 0.6g

The bread crust for this delicious lemon salmon requires only
a cheese grater and some ready-to-bake ciabatta.

Lemon-crusted Salmon with Tzatziki

ready-to-bake ciabatta bread
grated zest of 1 lemon
4 skinless salmon fillets,
about 175g/6oz each
1 egg, beaten

TO SERVE
2 × 170g tubs tzatziki
12 large black olives, stoned and
roughly chopped

Takes 30–35 minutes • Serves 4

1 Preheat the oven to 220°C/Gas 7/fan oven 200°C. Put a non-stick baking tray in the oven. Cut the bread in half and grate with the coarse part of the grater to make rough crumbs, discarding any hard crust. Tip the crumbs onto a plate and mix with the lemon zest.
2 Season the fish and dip the top and sides of each piece in the egg, then the crumbs. Put the fish on the heated tray and bake for 10–12 minutes, until cooked and crisp.
3 To serve, mix the tzatziki with the olives and season to taste. Divide the salmon between four plates and drizzle with the tzatziki.

• Per serving 506 kcalories, protein 44g, carbohydrate 21g, fat 28g, saturated fat 7.3g, fibre 1.5g, added sugar none, salt 2.56g

An intriguing new idea for smoked salmon. This recipe is a well-balanced meal in itself, so you don't need to serve anything with it.

Pan-fried Smoked Salmon with Beans

350g/12oz new potatoes, halved
200g/8oz fine green beans, topped and tailed
dash of olive oil
150g pack smoked salmon

FOR THE DRESSING
1 tsp Dijon mustard
1 tsp golden caster sugar
2 tbsp white wine vinegar
2 tbsp vegetable oil
2 tbsp olive oil
handful of snipped fresh chives

Takes 25–30 minutes • Serves 2

1 Make the dressing in a large bowl. Mix together the mustard and sugar, then stir in the vinegar and gradually whisk in the vegetable oil and olive oil until they are completely mixed. Stir in the chives. Set aside.
2 Cook the potatoes in a large pan of boiling salted water for 8–10 minutes until just undercooked, add the beans and continue to cook for 4–5 minutes until the beans and potatoes are done. Drain the vegetables and toss with most of the dressing.
3 Heat a dash of olive oil in a large non-stick frying pan until very hot and 'flash fry' the salmon for a moment until it just changes colour. Pile the beans and potatoes onto plates, lay the salmon on top, then drizzle with the remaining dressing.

• Per serving 488 kcalories, protein 24g, carbohydrate 34g, fat 29g, saturated fat 4g, fibre 4g, added sugar 3g, salt 3.83g

A classic Venetian dish that's so simple but so glamorous.
You can use plaice or lemon sole if you find sea bass a bit pricey.

Sea Bass with an Almond Crust

2 sea bass fillets,
about 175g/6oz each
1 little softened butter
2 rounded tbsp toasted flaked
almonds
1 shallot, finely chopped
150ml/¼ pint fresh fish stock
(from a carton)
small pinch of saffron strands
3 tbsp crème fraîche

Takes 20 minutes • Serves 2

1 Preheat the oven to 190°C/Gas 5/fan oven 170°C. Season the fish and spread a little butter over the flesh side of each fillet. Put in a shallow, buttered, ovenproof dish and sprinkle with the flaked almonds, lightly pressing them on. Bake for 12–15 minutes until the flesh flakes easily.

2 Meanwhile, make the sauce. Gently fry the shallot with a small knob of butter in a small pan. Add the stock and saffron, bring to the boil, then boil until reduced by about two-thirds. Stir in the crème fraîche and bubble for a minute or so until slightly thickened. Pour a little sauce around each portion of fish.

• Per serving 375 kcalories, protein 38g, carbohydrate 2g, fat 24g, saturated fat 8g, fibre 1g, added sugar none, salt 0.61g

An irresistibly creamy dish that's also really straightforward
to prepare and cook.

Poached Salmon with Mustard Sauce

2 slices of lemon
4 salmon fillets, about
140g/5oz each, skin on

FOR THE CARAMELISED ONIONS
25g/1oz butter
2 tsp vegetable oil
2 onions, roughly chopped
1 tsp muscovado sugar
350g bag prepared spinach leaves

FOR THE SAUCE
200ml carton crème fraîche
1 tbsp Dijon mustard
1 tbsp capers, drained, rinsed and
roughly chopped
small handful of fresh dill (ferns and
soft stalk tips), chopped

Takes 35–45 minutes • Serves 4

1 To caramelise the onions, melt the butter with the oil in a large pan and cook the onions and sugar over a low to medium heat for 20–25 minutes until soft and caramelised.
2 Meanwhile, make the sauce. Bring the crème fraîche to a gentle simmer in a small pan, stirring over a low heat. Stir in the mustard, capers and dill and simmer gently for 4–5 minutes, stirring now and again. Set aside.
3 Pour boiling water into a flameproof casserole to come 8cm/3in up the sides. Add the lemon and salt and bring back to the boil. Turn off the heat. Add the salmon, skin-side down. Cover and leave for 7 minutes.
4 Increase the heat under the onions, add the spinach and stir until wilted. Reheat the sauce. Serve the salmon on top of the onions and spinach and spoon the sauce over.

• Per serving 523 kcalories, protein 34g, carbohydrate 10g, fat 39g, saturated fat 16g, fibre 3g, added sugar 1g, salt 1.29g

Not only is this dish an appetising main course,
it's also high in omega-3 fatty acids.

Crunchy-topped Haddock

1 tbsp olive oil, plus extra
for drizzling
4 skinless unsmoked haddock fillets,
about 140g/5oz each
2 handfuls cherry tomatoes
3 tbsp mayonnaise
1 tsp garlic paste or 1 garlic clove,
crushed
100g/4oz white breadcrumbs
zest and juice 1 lemon
2 handfuls fresh flatleaf parsley,
roughly chopped

Takes 25 minutes • Serves 4

1 Preheat the oven to 220°C/Gas 7/fan oven 200°C. Lightly oil a large baking tray, then lay the haddock and tomatoes alongside each other. In a small bowl, mix the mayonnaise with the garlic paste or crushed garlic, then spread evenly over the fish.

2 In a separate bowl, toss together the breadcrumbs, lemon zest, juice and parsley, and season to taste. Top the fish with the breadcrumb mixture. Drizzle olive oil over the fish and tomatoes, and bake for 15 minutes or until the fish flakes slightly when pressed and the crust is golden and crunchy.

• Per serving 324 kcalories, protein 30g, carbohydrate 21g, fat 14g, saturated fat 2g, fibre 1g, added sugar none, salt 0.87g

This lightly spiced salmon is perfect to roast at the last moment. It's particularly good served as part of a buffet.

Roast Salmon with Spiced Coconut

50g/2oz butter
8 green cardamom pods, seeds removed and finely crushed
3 tbsp desiccated coconut
1 plump fresh red chilli, seeded and finely chopped
1 tbsp grated fresh root ginger
2 garlic cloves, finely chopped
1 tsp ground coriander
generous pinch of turmeric
8 slim boneless, skinless salmon fillets
2 tbsp finely chopped fresh coriander

Takes 30–40 minutes • Serves 8

1 Melt the butter in a medium pan, add the cardamom and coconut and stir constantly for 2–3 minutes until the coconut starts to toast. Stir in the chilli, ginger, garlic, ground coriander and turmeric. Cook for another minute, then leave to cool.

2 Arrange the salmon in a single layer, spaced slightly apart, in one large or two smaller buttered ovenproof dishes. Scatter on the coriander and spread the coconut mixture on top. Cook straight away, or cover with cling film and chill (for up to a day) until 1 hour before cooking.

3 Preheat the oven to 200°C/Gas 6/fan oven 180°C. Roast the salmon, uncovered, for 13–15 minutes until cooked, but still moist. Bring to the table in the dish(es).

• Per serving 254 kcalories, protein 26g, carbohydrate 1g, fat 16g, saturated fat 6g, fibre 1g, added sugar none, salt 0.15g

A delicious dish to serve at Christmas when you need a break from turkey. Do use raw prawns as they are much juicier than cooked ones.

Festive Fish Pie

200g/8oz smoked salmon
4 plum tomatoes, skinned, seeded
400g/14oz raw king prawns,
defrosted, patted dry
and peeled, with tails left on
500g/1lb 2oz skinless cod fillet,
cut into 2.5cm/1in chunks
2.5cm/1in piece of fresh root ginger
50g/2oz butter
50g/2oz plain flour
425ml/¾ pint milk
150ml/¼ pint dry vermouth
142ml carton single cream
3 tbsp chopped fresh dill
juice of ½ lime

FOR THE TOPPING
700g/1lb 9oz potatoes, peeled
good pinch of saffron strands
25g/1oz butter

Takes 1½–1¾ hours • Serves 6

1 Cut the salmon into strips and chop the tomatoes. Mix these with the prawns and cod in a buttered 3 litre/5¼ pint ovenproof dish.
2 Chop the ginger. Bring the butter, ginger, flour, milk and vermouth to the boil in a non-stick pan, whisking all the time until thickened and smooth. Reduce the heat and simmer for 2 minutes, then season and leave to cool, stirring occasionally. When cooled to room temperature, stir in the cream, dill and lime juice. Taste and season. Pour over the fish.
3 Slice the potatoes and boil in a pan of water with the saffron and some salt until just tender, then drain. Meanwhile, preheat the oven to 200°C/Gas 6/fan oven 180°C.
4 Arrange the potatoes, overlapping, over the pie mixture. Melt the butter and brush over. Bake for 30–40 minutes until golden.

• Per serving 493 kcalories, protein 42g, carbohydrate 34g, fat 17g, saturated fat 11g, fibre 2g, added sugar none, salt 2.7g

Court bouillon is a classic poaching liquor that's best used for poaching whole fish like salmon, or chunky fillets or steaks.

Salmon with Pepper and Basil Sauce

1 salmon, 1.5–2kg/3lb 5oz–4lb 8oz,
gutted, washed and trimmed,
head removed

FOR THE COURT BOUILLON
250ml/9fl oz dry white wine
3 tbsp white wine vinegar
1 small lemon and 1 onion, sliced
1 carrot, chopped
2 bay leaves
2 sprigs each tarragon and thyme
½ tsp whole black peppercorns

FOR THE SAUCE
2 roasted red peppers from a jar
1 shallot, finely chopped
5 tbsp olive oil
6 sprigs of fresh basil
1 tbsp sherry vinegar
100ml/3½fl oz dry white wine

Takes 1½ hours plus resting • Serves 6

1 Weigh the fish and calculate the cooking time at 30 minutes per kg/13 minutes per lb. Season inside and place in a roasting pan. Preheat oven to 160°C/Gas 3/fan oven 140°C.
2 Make the court bouillon. Place all the ingredients in a pan with 1.5 litres/2½ pints cold water. Bring to the boil, simmer for 20 minutes, then strain over the fish. Cover tightly with foil and poach in the oven for 45 minutes.
3 To make the sauce, drain and chop the peppers and sauté with the shallot in oil for 5 minutes. Chop the basil stems, add with the vinegar and wine, season, and simmer for 10 minutes. Finally, add some torn basil leaves.
4 Remove the fish from the oven, uncover but leave in the liquor for 15 minutes. Lift onto a board. Peel off the skin, scrape away the brown flesh. Serve with the sauce on top.

• Per serving 439 kcalories, protein 32g, carbohydrate 3g, fat 29g, saturated fat 5g, fibre 1g, added sugar none, salt 0.57g

These parcels can be prepared ahead of time and
left in the fridge until you're ready to cook.

Herby Almond Plaice Parcels

8 small plaice fillets, about 100g/4oz
each, skin on
2 lemons, peel and white pith
removed, very thinly sliced
2 handfuls of fresh mixed herbs
(tarragon, dill and parsley), finely
chopped
50g/2oz roasted flaked almonds
4 tbsp olive oil

Takes 30 minutes • Serves 4

1 Preheat the oven to 220°C/Gas 7/fan
oven 200°C. Put 4 plaice fillets, skin-side
down, in a roasting pan. Season, then top
with the lemon slices and mixed herbs and
finish with the almonds.
2 Cover the herb mixture with the remaining
plaice fillets, skin-side up, season the
skin and drizzle with olive oil. Bake for
15–20 minutes until the fish flakes easily.

• Per serving 340 kcalories, protein 36g, carbohydrate
2g, fat 21g, saturated fat 3g, fibre 1g, added sugar
none, salt 1g

This dish comes from southern Italy and relies on the
Mediterranean rule of good ingredients, simply cooked.

Italian-style Bass

750g/1lb 10oz waxy potatoes,
such as Charlotte
butter or oil, for greasing
6 sea bass fillets, about
175–200g/6–8oz each, skin on
250g pack cherry tomatoes
handful of black Italian olives
4–5 tbsp fish stock (preferably fresh,
from the chiller cabinet)
4–5 tbsp dry white wine
fresh basil, to serve

Takes 35–40 minutes • Serves 6

1 Preheat the oven to 190°C/Gas 5/fan
oven 170°C. Slice the potatoes and boil
for 6–8 minutes until just tender, then drain.
2 Butter or oil one large or two smaller,
shallow ovenproof dishes that will fit the fish
fillets in one layer (a roasting tin would work
well). Scatter the potatoes over the base
of the dishes, then halve the tomatoes and
scatter on top, along with the olives. Set
the fish fillets among the other ingredients,
then pour over the stock and wine and
season to taste.
3 Cover the dishes with foil and seal the
edges. Bake for 15 minutes until the fish is
tender. Serve scattered with basil.

• Per serving 287 kcalories, protein 37g, carbohydrate
23g, fat 5g, saturated fat 1g, fibre 2g, added sugar
none, salt 0.61g

Serve beer or a gewürztraminer wine from Alsace
with this easy and exotic dish.

Salmon with Thai Coconut Rice

2 tbsp light olive oil
25g/1oz butter
2 shallots, finely chopped
90g jar Thai red curry paste
grated zest of 1 lime
20g pack fresh coriander, stalks finely chopped, and leaves left whole
500g/1lb 2oz basmati rice
2 × 400ml cans coconut milk
4 kaffir lime leaves
6 skinless salmon fillets, about 140g/5oz each
juice of 2 limes
3 tbsp soy sauce
2 tsp golden caster sugar
4 spring onions, thinly sliced
1 plump fresh red chilli, seeded and finely chopped
lime wedges, to serve

Takes 1–1¼ hours • Serves 6

1 Heat the oil and butter in a wide, deep pan that will hold the salmon in one layer, then fry the shallots gently until golden (about 5 minutes). Stir in the curry paste and cook for 1 minute. Remove from the heat and add the lime zest, coriander stalks, rice and some salt. Mix well, then stir in the coconut milk and a canful of water. Bring to the boil, add the lime leaves and simmer for 5 minutes.
2 Stir the rice and lay the salmon on top. Cover and poach on the lowest heat for 15–20 minutes. Meanwhile, mix the lime juice with the soy sauce and sugar. In a separate bowl, mix the coriander leaves with the spring onions and chilli. Leave the fish and rice to stand off the heat for 5 minutes. Serve sprinkled with the spring onion mixture and dressing, with lime wedges for squeezing.

• Per serving 857 kcalories, protein 38g, carbohydrate 74g, fat 48g, saturated fat 24g, fibre none, added sugar 2g, salt 2.55g

The distinctive taste of this oily-textured fish works brilliantly with Asian flavours, including garlic, spices, ginger and soy sauce.

Orange-glazed Mackerel

2 × 300g/10oz mackerel, filleted and skin on, or 4 × 85g/3oz mackerel fillets, skin on
2 tbsp plain flour
½ tsp paprika, preferably smoked
2 tbsp extra-virgin olive oil
grated zest and juice of 1 small orange
1–2 tsp harissa paste, to taste
50g/2oz pine nuts, toasted
small bunch of fresh coriander, very roughly chopped

Takes 20 minutes • Serves 2

1 Roll the mackerel fillets in the flour sifted with the paprika and some seasoning. Shake off the excess and set the fish aside.
2 Put 1 tablespoon of the oil in a small bowl and whisk in the orange zest and juice and the harissa paste. Heat the remaining oil in a frying pan until very hot. Fry the fish fillets for 5 minutes, first on the skin side, then on the flesh side.
3 When the fish is nearly cooked (it should look firm), pour over the orange glaze. Bring to the boil and allow to bubble until sticky. Sprinkle over the pine nuts and coriander.

• Per serving 671 kcalories, protein 34g, carbohydrate 16g, fat 53g, saturated fat 8g, fibre 1g, added sugar none, salt 0.29g

Red mullet is a white, flaky-textured fish with an exquisite taste. It's delicious with herbs such as tarragon, rosemary and sage.

Roast Red Mullet with Pancetta

4 × 350g/12oz red mullet, scaled and gutted, or 8 × 100g/4oz red mullet fillets
small bunch of fresh tarragon, leaves roughly chopped
3 tbsp olive oil
1 garlic clove, crushed
100g/4oz diced pancetta or smoked bacon
1 red onion, thinly sliced
2 tbsp balsamic vinegar

Takes 35 minutes • Serves 4

1 Preheat the oven to 200°C/Gas 6/fan oven 180°C. Slash the red mullet through the flesh to the bone 3–4 times on each side. Mix the tarragon with 2 tablespoons of the oil and the garlic, season lightly, then brush over the fish, taking care to push some of the tarragon into the slashes. Leave to marinate for 10 minutes.
2 Put the pancetta and onion into a large roasting tin, drizzle with the remaining oil and roast for 5–7 minutes or until beginning to soften. Arrange the fish on top and drizzle with the vinegar. Roast for 12–15 minutes or until the fish is cooked; the flesh will flake when gently prodded.

• Per serving 279 kcalories, protein 24g, carbohydrate 4g, fat 19g, saturated fat 5g, fibre 1g, added sugar none, salt 1.50g

This versatile recipe is perfect for a light and healthy brunch for friends.

Salmon and Asparagus with New Potatoes

600g/1lb 5oz new potatoes, scrubbed and cut into chunks
175g/6oz asparagus, each piece cut into three
2 tbsp olive oil
2 × 140g/5oz salmon fillets, skinned and cut into large chunks
100g/4oz ripe cherry tomatoes, halved
1 tbsp snipped fresh chives
4 eggs

Takes 45 minutes • Serves 4

1 Cook the potatoes in boiling salted water for 5–8 minutes, or until just tender. Just before the potatoes are ready, tip in the asparagus and cook for 1 minute only. Drain well.

2 Heat the oil in a deep 23–25cm/9–10in frying pan. Add the potatoes and asparagus, shaking the pan gently so they spread out in one even layer. Cook for 1–2 minutes.

3 Make some gaps in the potatoes and asparagus and tuck in the salmon and tomatoes. Cover with a lid and cook for 1–2 minutes until the salmon is half-cooked. Take the lid off and scatter the chives over. Beat the eggs with salt and pepper, then pour over all the ingredients in the pan. Cover and leave for 4–5 minutes for the eggs to cook.

4 Preheat the grill to high. Place the pan under for 3 minutes or until the top is golden.

• Per serving 377 kcalories, protein 25g, carbohydrate 26g, fat 20g, saturated fat 4g, fibre 3g, added sugar none, salt 0.33g

Based on a Swedish recipe, this dish
is a really creamy treat.

Gravadlax Temptation

800g/1lb 12oz floury potatoes, such
as Maris Piper or King Edward
large knob of butter
2 onions, finely chopped
200g/8oz gravadlax, cut into thin
strips
284ml carton double cream
150ml/¼ pint milk

Takes about 1½ hours • Serves 4

1 Peel the potatoes and cut into very thin
chips using a mandolin (or slice thinly, stack
and cut through into sticks). Put the chips in
a bowl of cold salted water. Set aside.
2 Preheat the oven to 190°C/Gas 5/fan oven
170°C. Melt half the butter in a heavy pan and
fry the onions gently for 5 minutes. Butter a
shallow baking dish, about 1.2 litre/2 pint
capacity. Drain the potatoes and spread one-
third over the bottom of the dish. Season, then
scatter over half the gravadlax and onions.
Cover with another third of the potatoes, then
the remaining gravadlax and onions. Top with
the remaining potatoes and season well.
3 Warm the cream and milk to simmering
point, pour over the potatoes and dot with
the remaining butter. Bake for 1 hour or until
the potatoes are tender and the top is golden.

• Per serving 630 kcalories, protein 18g, carbohydrate
36g, fat 47g, saturated fat 25g, fibre 3g, added sugar
none, salt 2.33g

A superhealthy idea for a quick
family supper.

Warm Potato and Tuna Salad

650g/1lb 7oz new potatoes, halved
lengthways if large
2 tbsp pesto
4 tbsp olive oil
8 cherry tomatoes
200g can tuna
200g/8oz green beans, halved
couple of handfuls of baby spinach
leaves

Takes 20–30 minutes • Serves 4

1 Cook the potatoes in boiling water for
15 minutes or until tender.
2 Meanwhile, mix the pesto and oil to
make a dressing. Halve the tomatoes,
and drain and flake the tuna. Add the beans
to the potatoes for the last 3 minutes of
cooking time.
3 Drain the potatoes and beans and tip
into a salad bowl. Stir in the spinach so
that it wilts a little in the warmth from the
vegetables. Season with salt and pepper.
Scatter the tomatoes and tuna on top,
drizzle with the pesto and gently toss
everything together.

• Per serving 349 kcalories, protein 15g, carbohydrate
29g, fat 20g, saturated fat 3g, fibre 3g, added sugar
none, salt 0.71g

Buy locally caught fish, if you can,
for this healthy supper choice.

Whiting in a Bag

2 × 340g/12oz whiting, gutted
25g/1oz butter
2 tbsp chopped fresh dill
1 lemon, thinly sliced

Takes 20 minutes • Serves 2

1 Preheat the oven to 220°C/Gas 7/fan oven 190°C. Cut out two 40cm/6in diameter circles of baking parchment. Fold each piece in half and crease down the centre. Slash the fish 3–4 times on each side to the bone and set aside.

2 Melt the butter in a pan, add the dill and season. Put each fish on one half of the paper circles and tuck the lemon around. Drizzle the flavoured butter over the top and wrap each to form a parcel.

3 Put on baking sheets and bake for 12 minutes. To test if cooked, insert a skewer through the paper into the fish, leave for 15 seconds, then feel whether the tip is hot.

• Per serving 286 kcalories, protein 43g, carbohydrate 2g, fat 12g, saturated fat 7g, fibre 1g, added sugar none, salt 0.72g

An easy, no-fuss, no-butter-sauce version
of the classic fish pie.

Light and Fresh Fish Pie

450g/1lb new potatoes, thinly sliced
1 tbsp olive oil, plus 1 tsp
200g/8oz broccoli, broken into very
small florets
50g/2oz plain flour
600ml/1 pint skimmed milk
250g/9oz skinless salmon fillet, cut
into large chunks
250g/9oz skinless cod fillet, cut into
large chunks
3 tbsp chopped fresh parsley
finely grated zest of ½ lemon

Takes 50–65 minutes • Serves 4

1 Preheat the oven to 190°C/Gas 5/fan
oven 170°C and grease a 1.8 litre/3 pint
baking dish. Cook the potato slices in boiling
salted water for 3 minutes. Drain, return to
the pan and drizzle over 1 teaspoon oil to
stop the slices sticking.
2 Cover the broccoli in boiling water for
30 seconds, drain into a sieve and run under
the cold tap. Put the flour in a non-stick
saucepan with the milk and 1 tablespoon oil.
Bring to the boil over a low heat, stirring
vigorously with a wooden spoon, then cook
for a minute or two. Take off the heat, stir in
the broccoli, fish, parsley and lemon zest and
season with salt and pepper.
3 Tip the mixture into the dish, cover with
potato slices and season with pepper. Bake
for 30 minutes until golden.

• Per serving 377 kcalories, protein 35g, carbohydrate
36g, fat 11g, saturated fat 2g, fibre 3g, added sugar
none, salt 0.42g

In the summer, cook the tuna on the
barbecue, marinated in some oil first.

Tuna Steaks with Cucumber Relish

3 tbsp olive oil
4 tuna steaks, about 140g/5oz each

FOR THE RELISH
½ cucumber
2 spring onions, finely chopped
1 tomato, finely chopped
½ large fresh red chilli, seeded and
finely chopped
1 tbsp olive oil
2 tbsp chopped fresh parsley
1 tbsp lime or lemon juice

Takes 25–30 minutes • Serves 4

1 Put the oil into a food bag and add the
tuna steaks. Rub well together and leave for
30 minutes while you make the relish. Peel
the cucumber, halve lengthways and scoop
out the seeds. Chop the flesh into a small
dice. Mix with the rest of the ingredients and
seasoning to taste. Set aside.
2 Heat a cast iron ridged griddle pan until
hot, then cook the steaks for 2 minutes on
each side. Meaty fish is best served slightly
'pink'. Remove the steaks from the heat,
allow to stand for 3–5 minutes, then spoon
over the relish and serve.

• Per serving 271 kcalories, protein 34g, carbohydrate
2g, fat 14g, saturated fat 3g, fibre 1g, added sugar
none, salt 0.18g

A rich, smoky and satisfying lunchtime dish
that will keep you going all day.

Smoked Haddock One-Pot

450g/1lb skinned smoked haddock
fillet (undyed is best)
1 bay leaf
850ml/1½ pints milk
25g/1oz butter
1 onion, finely chopped
1 tbsp plain flour
1 garlic clove, crushed
1 red pepper, seeded and roughly
chopped
125ml/4fl oz dry sherry
pinch of paprika
225g/8oz floury potatoes, peeled
and diced
100g/4oz frozen or canned
sweetcorn kernels

TO SERVE
fresh parsley, chopped
hot garlic bread

Takes 35–40 minutes • Serves 4

1 Put the fish in a frying pan with the bay leaf and milk. Bring to a simmer, then cover and set aside for 10 minutes. Lift out the fish with a slotted spoon, flake roughly, discarding any bones, and strain the milk.
2 Melt the butter in a frying pan and cook the onion over a low heat for 3 minutes until softened. Sprinkle in the flour and stir for a minute. Add the garlic and red pepper and cook for 5 minutes. Stir in the sherry and simmer until almost all the liquid has gone.
3 Add the paprika and potatoes, pour in the poaching milk and bring to the boil. Cover and simmer for 15 minutes, add the sweetcorn and cook for 5 minutes more. Remove from the heat and gently fold in the fish. To serve, scatter over some chopped fresh parsley and accompany with garlic bread.

• Per serving 386 kcalories, protein 32g, carbohydrate 35g, fat 10g, saturated fat 6g, fibre 2g, added sugar none, salt 2.63g

A hearty main course that's also superhealthy. Roasting intensifies the peppers' sweetness while keeping the fish moist in the juice.

Zesty Roast Salmon and Cod

800g/1lb 12oz thick, boneless, skinless salmon fillet, cut into 8
800g/1lb 12oz thick, boneless, skinless cod loin, cut into 8
3 tbsp olive oil
grated zest and juice of 2 oranges
85g/3oz raisins
3 red peppers, halved, seeded and each half cut into 3
3 orange peppers, halved, seeded and each half cut into 3
50g/2oz pine nuts
large handful of fresh flatleaf parsley, roughly chopped

Takes about 45 minutes, plus marinating • Serves 8

1 Put the fish in a large bowl, add 2 tablespoons of the oil, the orange zest and season. Carefully toss the fish to coat, cover and leave to marinate in the fridge for 1–2 hours. Put the raisins into a small bowl, pour over the orange juice and set aside. Preheat the oven to 200°C/Gas 6/fan oven 180°C.
2 Place the peppers in a large shallow roasting tray and drizzle with the remaining oil. Season, toss together and roast for 30 minutes. Toast the pine nuts on a separate tray in the oven for 8–10 minutes until golden.
3 Arrange the fish and raisins on top of the peppers and pour over the juices. Scatter the pine nuts over and season with a good pinch of salt. Cook in the oven for 12–15 minutes until the fish is just cooked through. Scatter with parsley before serving.

• Per serving 407 kcalories, protein 41g, carbohydrate 15g, fat 21g, saturated fat 3g, fibre 2g, added sugar none, salt 0.3g

Smoked trout is a good alternative to smoked salmon. This recipe is healthy, super-quick and a great way of using up leftover potatoes.

Smoked Trout Salad

120g bag salad leaves (rocket, spinach and watercress is a good mix)
250g/9oz small new potatoes, boiled and halved
8–10 radishes, trimmed and quartered
175g/6oz cooked beetroot, drained and cut into wedges
2 smoked trout or mackerel fillets
1 tsp hot horseradish sauce
2 tbsp half-fat crème fraîche
splash of milk

Takes 15–20 minutes • Serves 2

1 Pile the salad leaves on two plates and divide the potatoes, radishes and beetroot between them. Flake over the smoked trout.
2 Mix the horseradish and crème fraîche with enough milk to make a runny dressing. Season and drizzle over the salad.

• Per serving 254 kcalories, protein 19g, carbohydrate 31g, fat 6g, saturated fat 2g, fibre 4g, added sugar none, salt 1.76g

A satisfying and delicious dish
that can be whipped up in no time.

Seafood Spaghetti

175g/6oz spaghetti
1 tbsp olive oil
2 garlic cloves, finely chopped
400g can chopped tomatoes
200g jar of cockles in vinegar,
drained
pinch of dried chilli flakes
2 tbsp chopped fresh parsley

Takes 15 minutes • Serves 2
(easily doubled)

1 Cook the spaghetti in a pan of salted boiling water for 10–12 minutes until tender.
2 Meanwhile, heat the oil in a frying pan, then fry the garlic for 30 seconds. Add the tomatoes and bubble for 2–3 minutes. Add the cockles and chilli flakes, season, then stir to heat through.
3 Drain the spaghetti and return to the pan. Stir in the sauce and serve sprinkled with chopped parsley.

• Per serving 424 kcalories, protein 21g, carbohydrate 71g, fat 8g, saturated fat 1g, fibre 5g, added sugar none, salt 1.39g

A smart yet simple supper dish that's low in fat, too. You can make the dressing in advance, then refrigerate it until you're ready to serve.

Smoked Salmon and Avocado

2 ripe avocados
juice of 1 lemon
250g pack smoked salmon
small handful of fresh tarragon,
leaves only, chopped
4 tbsp crème fraîche
1 tbsp capers, drained
wholemeal or soda bread, to serve

Takes 20–25 minutes • Serves 6

1 Stone and peel the avocados, cut the flesh into chunks and toss in half the lemon juice. Twist and fold the smoked salmon pieces onto serving plates, then scatter with the avocado.

2 Mix together the tarragon, crème fraîche and remaining lemon juice. Drizzle over the salmon, scatter with the capers and serve straight away, with the wholemeal or soda bread.

• Per serving 153 kcalories, protein 12g, carbohydrate 1g, fat 11g, saturated fat 2g, fibre 1g, added sugar none, salt 2.17g

Add 150g/6oz cooked, peeled prawns
for more seafood flavour.

Smoked Haddock Risotto

2 smoked haddock fillets, about
200g/8oz each
1 leek, trimmed and sliced
small knob of butter
300g/10oz risotto rice
3 tbsp mascarpone
handful of snipped chives, to serve

Takes 30 minutes • Serves 4

1 Put the fish in a large bowl, cover with
1.2 litres/2 pints boiling water and leave
for 8–10 minutes until the fish flakes easily.
Remove with a slotted spoon, peel off the
skin and flake into large chunks, discarding
any bones. Keep the warm liquid.
2 Melt the butter in a large frying pan and
cook the leek until softened. Stir in the rice,
then pour over the fish poaching liquid. Stir
well then leave to bubble for 15–20 minutes
until the rice is nearly cooked.
3 Carefully fold the fish flakes into the
rice without breaking them up. Cook for
2 minutes more, stirring occasionally, until
most of the liquid has evaporated. Stir in the
mascarpone and sprinkle with the chives
just before serving.

• Per serving 397 kcalories, protein 26g, carbohydrate
60g, fat 8g, saturated fat 4g, fibre 2g, added sugar
none, salt 2g

Any oily fish works well for this recipe, but sardines are
a particularly good source of omega-3 fatty acids.

Sardines and Watercress on Toast

2 slices of granary bread
1 garlic clove, halved
1 ripe tomato, thinly sliced
115g can Portuguese sardines in
spring water, drained
large handful of organic watercress
or wild rocket
splash of balsamic vinegar

Takes 10 minutes • Serves 2

1 Lightly toast the bread. Rub the cut side
of the garlic over the surface of the toast
and arrange the tomato slices on top.
Add seasoning if you want to.
2 Break up the sardines with a fork and
arrange on top. Pile on the watercress and
drizzle with balsamic vinegar.

• Per serving 202 kcalories, protein 15g, carbohydrate
23g, fat 6g, saturated fat 1g, fibre 3g, added sugar
none, salt 0.85g

A clever low-fat recipe that doesn't compromise on taste.

Smoked Haddock with Rocket and Rice

225g/8½oz basmati rice
450ml/12fl oz fish or vegetable stock
(a cube is fine)
350g/12oz skinned smoked
haddock (undyed is best)
150g pack sugar snap peas
3 spring onions, finely sliced
150g pack cherry tomatoes, halved
50g bag rocket

Takes 15–20 minutes • Serves 4

1 Put the rice and stock into a pan and bring to the boil. Cover, reduce to a simmer and cook for 6 minutes.
2 Cut the fish into chunks, arrange on the rice and cook for 2 minutes. Sprinkle with the sugar snaps and spring onions, cover and cook over a low heat for 2 minutes more.
3 Gently fork the tomatoes and rocket through the rice.

• Per serving 286 kcalories, protein 23g, carbohydrate 49g, fat 1g, saturated fat 1g, fibre 1g, added sugar none, salt 2.08g

A pie full of low-fat fishy goodness. Any type of white fish is low in fat and a good source of protein and vitamins.

Superhealthy Fish Pie

500g/1lb 2oz floury potatoes, peeled and cut into chunks
1 medium swede (weighing about 600g/1lb 5oz), cut into chunks
200g low-fat soft cheese with garlic and herbs
150ml/¼ pint vegetable stock
4 tsp cornflour, blended with 2 tbsp cold water
650g/1lb 7oz boneless, skinless cod, cut into large chunks
100g/4oz cooked peeled prawns
1 tbsp chopped fresh parsley

Takes 1–1¼ hours • Serves 4

1 Cook the potatoes and swede in boiling water until tender (about 20 minutes).
2 Preheat the oven to 190°C/Gas 5/fan oven 170°C. While the potatoes and swede cook, put the soft cheese and stock into a large saucepan and heat gently, stirring with a wooden spoon, until blended and smooth. Now add the blended cornflour and cook until thick.
3 Stir the fish into the sauce with the prawns and parsley. Season with some pepper.
4 Tip the mixture into a 1.5 litre/2½ pint baking dish. Drain the potatoes and swede, mash them well and season with some pepper. Spoon the mash over the fish to cover it completely. Bake for 25–30 minutes until piping hot, then transfer to a hot grill for a few minutes to brown the top.

• Per serving 359 kcalories, protein 45g, carbohydrate 36g, fat 5g, saturated fat none, fibre 5g, added sugar none, salt 1.34g

Lean white fish, such as haddock or whiting, is perfect for those on a diet or seeking to improve their health.

Mediterranean Fish Parcels

250g/9oz baby new potatoes, scrubbed
1 tsp olive oil
2 × 175g/6oz firm white fish fillets, such as haddock or whiting
2 tsp sun-dried tomato paste or tomato purée
finely grated zest of 1 lemon, plus 2 tsp lemon juice
about 10 black or green olives
1 tbsp capers, rinsed
2 sprigs of fresh rosemary or thyme

Takes 40–50 minutes • Serves 2

1 Preheat the oven to 190°C/Gas 5/fan oven 170°C. Boil the potatoes in salted water for about 12 minutes or until tender, then drain well.

2 Take two large sheets of foil, about 30cm/12in square, and brush the middle area of each sheet with olive oil. Put a fish fillet on top and spread with the tomato paste. Sprinkle with the lemon zest and juice, add the cooked potatoes, olives and capers, then season with ground pepper.

3 Top with a sprig of rosemary or thyme, then loosely wrap and secure each parcel tightly to completely enclose the ingredients. Put the parcels on a baking sheet and bake for 20–25 minutes, or until the fish flakes easily when tested with a fork.

• Per serving 275 kcalories, protein 35g, carbohydrate 21g, fat 6g, saturated fat 0.7g, fibre 1.9g, added sugar none, salt 1.33g

Try other smoked fish, including smoked-trout fillets or mackerel.

Hot-smoked Salmon and Potato Salad

500g/1lb 2 oz baby new potatoes, larger ones halved
2 handfuls of watercress
135–150g pack flaked hot-smoked salmon
3 spring onions, sliced
3 tbsp chopped fresh dill
4 rounded tbsp Greek yogurt

Takes 25–30 minutes • Serves 2

1 Steam or boil the potatoes for 15–20 minutes until tender, drain and cool for a few minutes. Put a handful of watercress on each plate. Scatter over the potatoes, salmon flakes, spring onions and half the dill.
2 Spoon the yogurt on top, scatter with the remaining dill, and season with black pepper. Mix at the table to serve. The warm potatoes will soften the yogurt into the dill to make a dressing.

• Per serving 354 kcalories, protein 25g, carbohydrate 43g, fat 11g, saturated fat 4g, fibre 4g, added sugar none, salt 1.93g

Fresh tuna has a lovely meaty texture that's even better when marinated before cooking.

Griddled Tuna with Bean Salad

2 fresh tuna steaks, about 175g/6oz each
1 tbsp olive oil
1 tbsp lemon juice
1 large garlic clove, crushed
1 tbsp chopped fresh rosemary leaves

FOR THE SALAD
410g can cannellini beans, drained and rinsed
8 cherry tomatoes, quartered
½ small red onion, thinly sliced
50g bag rocket
2 tbsp extra-virgin olive oil
1 tbsp lemon juice
1 tsp wholegrain mustard
1 tsp clear honey

Takes 30–40 minutes, plus marinating
• Serves 2

1 Put the tuna in a shallow dish, drizzle over the oil and lemon juice and scatter over the garlic and rosemary. Turn the tuna so it's well coated. Cover and leave in the fridge for at least 30 minutes.
2 Tip the beans into a large bowl. Toss in the tomatoes, onion and rocket. Put the oil, lemon juice, mustard, honey and some seasoning in a screw-top jar. Seal and set aside.
3 Heat a cast iron ridged grill pan or frying pan until very hot. Cook the tuna on a moderately high heat for 2 minutes on each side – don't overcook or it will be dry.
4 Shake the dressing. Pour over the salad and mix together. Serve the salad with the tuna on top.

• Per serving 565 kcalories, protein 54g, carbohydrate 30g, fat 26g, saturated fat 5g, fibre 9g, added sugar 2g, salt 0.67g

For a richer version, use a 190g jar of tuna in olive oil, reserving
1 tablespoon of the oil to drizzle over the pizza when you add the fish.

Ten-minute Tuna Pizza

23cm/9in thin-crust pizza base
1 tbsp tomato purée
1 garlic clove, sliced
handful of pitted black olives
large handful of cherry tomatoes,
halved
1 tbsp olive oil, for drizzling
1 tbsp capers, drained
200g can tuna in brine, drained and
flaked
handful of fresh basil leaves

Takes 10–15 minutes • Serves 2

1 Preheat the oven to 230°C/Gas 8/fan
oven 210°C. Spread the pizza base with
tomato purée. Scatter over the garlic,
olives, tomatoes and half the oil. Bake for
10 minutes until the tomatoes start to
change colour and the base is crisp.
2 Remove from the oven, sprinkle over
the capers, tuna and basil, drizzle with oil,
then serve.

• Per serving 322 kcalories, protein 25g, carbohydrate
38g, fat 9g, saturated fat 2g, fibre 2g, added sugar
1g, salt 2.65g

You'll find Mediterranean Tomato Rice – a flavoursome mixture of microwaveable summer veg and basmati rice – in supermarkets.

Prawn and Rice Salad

250g pouch Mediterranean Tomato Rice
1 large courgette, finely diced
250g pack frozen cooked jumbo tiger prawns, defrosted and patted dry
good handful of fresh basil leaves, torn
1 tsp lemon juice, plus extra for drizzling
1 tbsp olive oil, plus extra for drizzling
50–60g bag fresh salad leaves, to serve

Takes 10 minutes • Serves 2

1 Cook the rice according to packet instructions, then tip into a bowl. Toss in the courgette, prawns and basil, then moisten with the lemon juice and olive oil and season to taste.
2 Arrange a mix of salad leaves on each plate, drizzle with olive oil and lemon juice and spoon the rice salad on top.

• Per serving 403 kcalories, protein 34g, carbohydrate 38g, fat 13g, saturated fat 1g, fibre 9g, added sugar none, salt 6.45g

Canned tuna is one of those items you can't afford to be without in your storecupboard. Here tuna lifts a simple pasta dish and makes it special.

Tuna and Pea Pasta

300g/10oz dried pasta bows or
other small pasta shapes
140g/5oz frozen peas
1 tbsp olive oil
1 onion, chopped
4 smoked streaky bacon rashers,
roughly chopped
400g can chopped tomatoes
200g can tuna, drained and flaked
3 tbsp crème fraîche
splash of Tabasco

Takes 25 minutes • Serves 4

1 Cook the pasta in boiling salted for water for about 10 minutes, or according to packet instructions, until tender. Add the frozen peas for the last 3 minutes of the cooking time.
2 Meanwhile, heat the oil in a large pan and fry the onion and bacon for about 5 minutes until the onion is soft. Add the tomatoes, stir well and bring to the boil, then cover the pan and leave to simmer.
3 Drain the pasta and peas and add to the tomato sauce with the tuna. Gently stir in the crème fraîche and Tabasco, season with some salt and pepper, and serve hot.

• Per serving 473 kcalories, protein 26g, carbohydrate 65g, fat 14g, saturated fat 5.6g, fibre 5.6g, added sugar 0.1g, salt 1.24g

Bags of salad are a great idea when you want a quick meal, and this one has loads of delicious flavours, too.

Smoked Mackerel Salad

2 thick slices of crusty bread
1 tbsp olive oil
2 × 100g/4oz smoked mackerel fillets
150g bag salad leaves (beetroot, lamb's lettuce and red chard is a good mix)
2–3 tbsp ready-made Caesar salad dressing

Takes 20–25 minutes • Serves 2

1 Preheat the oven to 200°C/Gas 6/fan oven 180°C. Cut the bread into cubes (including the crusts) and toss with the oil on a baking sheet. Spread out evenly and bake for 15 minutes until golden and crunchy.
2 Remove the skin from the mackerel and flake the flesh into a large salad bowl. Add the salad leaves, dressing and croûtons and toss well to mix.

• Per serving 582 kcalories, protein 23g, carbohydrate 22g, fat 45g, saturated fat 8.4g, fibre 1.3g, added sugar 0.2g, salt 2.82g

This is a handy dish that takes little time
to prepare but always tastes great.

Pasta with Tuna and Tomato

2 tbsp olive oil
1 onion, chopped
2 garlic cloves, finely chopped
400g can chopped tomatoes with
herbs
½ tsp chilli powder
1 tsp sugar
500g packet pasta bows
100g can tuna, drained
handful of fresh basil leaves
(optional)

Takes 25 minutes • Serves 4

1 Heat the oil in a pan, add the onion and cook for a couple of minutes. Stir in the garlic, tomatoes, chilli and sugar. Season and bring to the boil. Stir, then reduce the heat and simmer for 5 minutes.
2 Meanwhile, bring a large pan of salted water to the boil. Add the pasta and cook according to packet instructions.
3 Flake the tuna into the sauce and heat through. Drain the pasta, return to the pan and stir in the sauce and basil leaves. Serve with a generous grinding of pepper.

• Per serving 556 kcalories, protein 22g, carbohydrate 101g, fat 10g, saturated fat 1.5g, fibre 5.3g, added sugar 1.3g, salt 0.41g

Tuna in oil is a great choice for salads and stir fries, as you can use some of the oil as a base for the dressing or to cook with.

Tuna and Chickpea Tabbouleh

100g/4oz couscous
200g can tuna in olive oil
410g can chickpeas, drained and rinsed
140g/5oz baby plum tomatoes, halved
¼ cucumber, cut into sticks
juice of ½ lemon
2 tbsp chopped fresh mint

Takes 20 minutes • Serves 2

1 Put the couscous in a large bowl and pour over 225ml/8fl oz boiling water. Cover and leave to stand for 5 minutes.
2 Drain the tuna, save the oil and flake the flesh. Fork through the couscous to separate the grains, add the tuna, chickpeas, tomatoes and cucumber and toss well to mix.
3 Make a dressing with the tuna oil, lemon juice, mint and some salt and pepper to taste. Pour over the tabbouleh, toss and serve.

• Per serving 424 kcalories, protein 35g, carbohydrate 48g, fat 12g, saturated fat 1.4g, fibre 5.9g, added sugar none, salt 1.3g

This main-course salad couldn't be easier – simply take a bag of frozen prawns out of the freezer and create this inspired recipe.

Prawn and Avocado Pasta Salad

400g bag penne pasta
400g bag frozen raw peeled tiger prawns, defrosted and patted dry
4 tbsp olive oil
grated zest and juice of 1 large lemon
1 small garlic clove, finely chopped
1 large avocado, peeled, stoned and cut into cubes
250g pack cherry tomatoes, halved
2 spring onions, thinly sliced
100g bag rocket
small bunch of fresh basil leaves, torn

Takes 20–25 minutes • Serves 4

1 Cook the pasta in boiling salted water for 10 minutes, or according to packet instructions, until tender. Just before the end, add the prawns and cook until they all turn pink. Drain, cool under cold water, drain again and transfer to a big bowl.
2 Put the oil, lemon zest and juice, garlic, avocado, tomatoes and spring onions in a separate bowl, then mix well – don't mash the avocado. Season. Gently toss the mix into the pasta, with the rocket and basil.

• Per serving 636 kcalories, protein 32g, carbohydrate 80g, fat 24g, saturated fat 3g, fibre 6g, added sugar none, salt 0.55 g

Bags of frozen seafood are really handy – just use the amount
you need and keep the rest for another time.

Chunky Chilli Seafood Stew

1 tbsp olive oil
1 small onion, chopped
1 garlic clove, crushed
1 pinch of fennel seeds or a splash
of Pernod, anisette or Ricard (not
essential but does add flavour)
1 small pinch of chilli flakes
1 very small pinch of saffron strands
5 new potatoes, sliced
125ml/4fl oz white wine
220g can chopped tomatoes
¼ fish stock cube
200g/8oz frozen seafood cocktail,
defrosted
handful of chopped fresh parsley
crusty bread, to serve

Takes 1 hour–1 hour 10 minutes •
Serves 1

1 Heat the olive oil in a medium saucepan
and fry the onion on a low heat for about
7–10 minutes, stirring occasionally, until very
soft and golden. Throw in the garlic, fennel
seeds (if using), chilli flakes, saffron strands
and the potatoes and continue to cook for a
couple of minutes, stirring.
2 Pour the wine, and the Pernod (if using),
into the saucepan and let it simmer for a
couple of minutes. Stir in the tomatoes and
two canfuls of water. Crumble in the quarter
of stock cube, season, mix well, and simmer
for 35 minutes, uncovered.
3 Stir in the seafood cocktail and simmer
for 3–4 minutes until everything is piping hot.
Scatter in the parsley, then serve straight
away with some crusty bread on the side.

• Per serving 524 kcalories, protein 43g, carbohydrate
36g, fat 15g, saturated fat 2g, fibre 5g, added sugar
none, salt 1.73g

This is a great recipe to experiment with – try tuna instead of salmon, and add chopped herbs, curry powder, lime juice or sliced spring onion.

Simple Salmon Fishcakes

10 cream crackers
198g can sweetcorn, drained
1 small onion, coarsely grated
6 tbsp mayonnaise, plus a little extra to serve
juice of ½ lemon
1 mugful of frozen peas, defrosted by pouring boiling water over them
418g can salmon, drained, skin removed, and flaked into large chunks
2 tbsp sunflower oil
watercress salad and lemon wedges, to serve

Take 25–35 minutes •
Makes 8 cakes (serves 4)

1 Break the crackers into a food processor, tip in the sweetcorn and blitz to a loose paste. Transfer the paste into a large bowl.
2 Mix the onion, mayonnaise and lemon juice into the paste until everything is bound together. Gently stir in the peas and flaked salmon, crushing any small bones with your fingers.
3 Shape the mixture into 8 cakes. Heat 1 tablespoon of the oil in a frying pan over a medium heat, add 4 fishcakes and fry for 4 minutes on each side until crisp and brown. Remove and drain on kitchen paper then repeat with the remaining oil and fishcakes. Serve with a watercress salad, extra mayonnaise and lemon wedges.

• Per serving 463 kcalories, protein 22g, carbohydrate 26g, fat 31g, saturated fat 6g, fibre 2g, added sugar 3g, salt 1.73g

You don't have to use smoked salmon – prawns, flaked smoked mackerel, trout or canned tuna work equally well.

Smoked Salmon Kedgeree

a knob of butter
1 bunch of spring or salad onions, trimmed and roughly chopped (white and green kept separate)
1 tbsp curry powder
400g/14oz basmati rice
700ml/1¼ pints hot chicken or vegetable stock
4 eggs
225g pack smoked salmon trimmings

Takes 35 minutes • Serves 4

1 Melt the butter in a large pan over a medium heat, add the white onions and curry powder and cook for a few minutes until the onions soften. Tip in the rice and stir to coat in the butter. Pour in the hot stock and bring to the boil. Stir once and boil for 5 minutes, then cover the pan and cook the rice on the lowest possible heat for 15 minutes.
2 While the rice is cooking, bring a small pan of water to simmering point. Lower in the eggs and simmer for 8 minutes. Move the pan to the sink and tip off the hot water, then fill the pan with cold water from the tap. Take out the eggs, then shell and roughly chop them.
3 Toss the rice in a serving dish with the smoked salmon and green onions. Taste for seasoning. Put the pieces of egg on top and gently fork them through.

• Per serving 537 kcalories, protein 31g, carbohydrate 82g, fat 12g, saturated fat 3.5g, fibre 1.2g, added sugar none, salt 3.55g

Easy, flavoursome and with interesting textures – delicious.

Peppered Mackerel and Noodle Supper

250g pack medium rice noodles
2 tbsp soy sauce
1 large garlic clove, crushed
small knob of fresh root ginger, grated
½ cucumber, halved and sliced
1 bunch of spring onions, sliced
handful of fresh coriander leaves
4 peppered smoked mackerel fillets, broken into large flakes

Takes 20 minutes • Serves 4

1 Boil a kettle of water and tip the noodles into a large heatproof bowl. Cover them with boiling water and leave for 5 minutes. Meanwhile, mix the soy sauce with the garlic, ginger and 3 tablespoons of water to make a dressing.
2 Drain the noodles, rinse under the cold tap, then drain them again. Tip into a bowl and toss in the cucumber, spring onions, half the coriander and half the dressing. Top each portion of noodles with mackerel, drizzle the remaining dressing over and sprinkle with the rest of the coriander. Serve.

• Per serving 663 kcalories, protein 28g, carbohydrate 54g, fat 39g, saturated fat 10g, fibre 1g, added sugar 0.1g, salt 4g

You can use any kind of canned tuna for this recipe – in brine, spring water or oil – but make sure it's dolphin-friendly.

Crusty Tuna Hash

500g/1lb 2oz new potatoes
1 tbsp vegetable oil
1 onion, chopped
1 tbsp korma curry paste
200g can tuna, drained and flaked
handful of chopped fresh coriander

Takes 30–35 minutes, plus cooling •
Serves 2

1 Cook the potatoes in boiling salted water for 15–20 minutes until tender. Drain and leave until cold.

2 Heat the oil in a large, non-stick frying pan and fry the onion until softened (about 5 minutes). Add the potatoes and curry paste and heat gently, crushing the potatoes with a fork.

3 Stir in the tuna and cook gently for a few minutes until a crust forms underneath, then stir and cook a few minutes more until another crust forms. Toss in the coriander just before serving.

• Per serving 419 kcalories, protein 27g, carbohydrate 46g, fat 15g, saturated fat 2g, fibre 3.4g, added sugar none, salt 0.96g

A fantastic quick fish supper that makes
the most of delicate Asian flavours.

Spicy Singaporean Fish

2 red chillies, seeded and chopped
2 shallots, chopped
1 garlic clove, chopped
1 lemongrass stalk, outer leaves
removed, chopped
small knob of fresh root ginger,
peeled and chopped
2 tsp soy sauce
pinch of sugar
2 tbsp vegetable oil
2 lemon sole fillets, about
120g/4½oz each
fresh chives and coriander, to serve

Takes 20 minutes • Serves 2

1 Make a paste by blending together the chillies, shallots, garlic, lemongrass, ginger, soy sauce and sugar in a blender or coffee grinder, or use a pestle and mortar. Heat the oil in a small frying pan and cook the paste for 2 minutes until it has darkened slightly and you can smell the spices. Season with a little salt if you like, then set aside.

2 Preheat the grill to medium. Put the fish onto the grill pan and use the back of a teaspoon to smear the paste all over the fleshy side, making a thin layer covering the whole fish. Cook under the grill for 10 minutes until the fish flakes easily. Serve straight away, garnished with chives and coriander.

• Per serving 213 kcalories, protein 22g, carbohydrate 3g, fat 13g, saturated fat 2g, fibre 0.3g, added sugar 1g, salt 1.2g

This tasty dish is perfect for picnics. Bake just before leaving home and double wrap the fish in foil as soon as it comes out of the oven.

Baked Sea Bass with Lemongrass

1 whole sea bass, about 1.3kg/3lb, gutted and cleaned
3 lemongrass stalks, cut diagonally into 2.5cm/1in pieces
2 small chillies, halved
2 garlic cloves, halved
4cm/½in piece of fresh root ginger, peeled and cut into thin strips
1 tsp clear honey
2 limes
2 tbsp olive oil, plus extra for oiling
2 kaffir lime leaves or 2–3 thin strips of lime zest

Takes 30–35 minutes • Serves 4

1 Preheat the oven to 200°C/Gas 6/fan oven 180°C. Wash the fish inside and out, and pat dry with kitchen paper. Score the skin 4–5 times on each side, then lay the fish on a sheet of oiled foil, big enough to wrap it loosely.
2 Bruise the lemongrass in a mortar with the chillies, garlic, ginger, honey, the juice of 1 lime and 1 tablespoon of the oil.
3 Season the fish inside and out. Mix half the pounded mixture with the last of the oil and rub over the fish, pushing it into the cuts.
4 Quarter the second lime and push 2 pieces into the cavity with the remainder of the pounded mixture and the lime leaves. Squeeze the juice from the last 2 lime quarters over the fish and make a loose parcel with the foil. Bake for 25 minutes. Leave it to rest for about 5 minutes before opening the parcel.

• Per serving 298 kcalories, protein 45g, carbohydrate 2g, fat 12g, saturated fat 1.9g, fibre 0.1g, added sugar 1g, salt 0.41g

If you can't find raw shell-on prawns,
use 175g/6oz peeled raw prawns.

Prawns with Green Mango Salad

2 tbsp lime juice
1 small red chilli, seeded and finely chopped
2 tbsp fish sauce
1 tbsp light muscovado sugar
3 shallots, finely sliced
85g/3oz roasted salted peanuts, finely chopped
2 green mangoes or 3 Granny Smith apples
2 tbsp chopped fresh mint
1 tbsp sunflower oil
200g pack raw shell-on headless prawns, peeled but with tails on
2 Little Gem lettuces
2 spring onions, shredded

Takes 20–25 minutes • Serves 4

1 Mix together the lime juice, chilli, fish sauce and sugar in a large bowl. Add the shallots and three-quarters of the peanuts and mix well. Cover and set aside for up to 4 hours.

2 Peel and coarsely grate the mango or apple, and stir into the mixture along with the mint. Heat the oil in a frying pan or wok, add the prawns and stir fry quickly until evenly pink (about 2 minutes).

3 Scatter the lettuce leaves on a serving plate and spoon the salad mixture into the centre. Surround with the prawns and scatter over the remaining peanuts and spring onions.

• Per serving 176 kcalories, protein 10g, carbohydrate 12g, fat 10g, saturated fat 2g, fibre 3g, added sugar 3g, salt 1.26g

You'll find dried rice noodles in your local supermarket. They work well in salads and stir-fries, and complement any seafood, veg or meat.

Prawn and Herb Noodle Salad

100g/4oz dried rice noodles (medium size)
1 small cucumber, cut into long strips
400g pack cooked peeled tiger prawns, defrosted and patted dry if frozen
small handful each of fresh coriander and mint leaves
6 tbsp olive oil
finely grated zest and juice of 1 lime
1 garlic clove, crushed
8 iceberg lettuce leaves, to serve

Takes 20–25 minutes • Serves 4

1 Soak the noodles in boiling water for 5 minutes, or according to packet instructions. Drain and rinse under the cold tap, then drain again and place in a large bowl with the cucumber and prawns.
2 Put the coriander and mint in a food processor with the remaining ingredients (except the lettuce) and blitz until fairly smooth. Season and toss with the noodle mixture. Serve in the lettuce leaves.

• Per serving 338 kcalories, protein 25g, carbohydrate 22g, fat 18g, saturated fat 2.5g, fibre 0.4g, added sugar none, salt 2.05g

Fried fish is popular in Vietnam and the staple ingredient
is fish sauce, available from good supermarkets.

Vietnamese Fried Fish

2 × 200g/8oz boneless monkfish
tails, skinned
4 garlic cloves, peeled
5cm/2in piece of galangal or fresh
root ginger, peeled and chopped
50ml/2fl oz Greek yogurt
1 tbsp turmeric
½ large onion, peeled
a little vegetable or sunflower oil,
for frying
dill fronds and lime slices, to garnish
boiled rice, to serve

FOR THE *NUOC CHAM* SAUCE
2 fresh plump red chillies, halved
3 garlic cloves
1 tbsp caster sugar
3 tbsp fish sauce
3 tbsp rice vinegar

Takes 30 minutes, plus marinating •
Serves 4

1 Slice the monkfish into discs. Blitz the
garlic and galangal or ginger in a food
processor, or pound in a mortar. Tip into
a shallow dish and stir in the yogurt and
turmeric. Stir in the fish, cover and leave
to marinate for up to 4 hours in the fridge.
2 Make the *nuoc cham*. Remove the
seeds from the chillies and pound with the
garlic and sugar in a mortar to make a
paste. Mix in the fish sauce, vinegar and
6 tablespoons water.
3 Very finely slice the onion. Heat some oil
in a large, heavy frying pan. Add the onion
and fry over a medium heat for 3–4 minutes,
until softened and pale golden. Add the
monkfish and fry for about 4 minutes, or until
browned. Sprinkle with the *nuoc cham*,
garnish with dill and lime, and serve with rice.

• Per serving 217 kcalories, protein 21g, carbohydrate
12g, fat 9g, saturated fat 1.7g, fibre 0.7g, added
sugar 4.5g, salt 5.23g

A wonderful, authentic Thai classic. If there are two thicknesses of noodle on offer, go for the thicker ones for this recipe.

Pad Thai

125g (½ × 250g pack) rice noodles
3 tbsp lime juice (about 2 limes)
½ tsp cayenne pepper
2 tsp light muscovado sugar
2 tbsp fish sauce
2 tbsp vegetable oil
200g/8oz cooked peeled tiger prawns, tails left on
4 spring onions, sliced
140g/5oz beansprouts
25g/1oz salted peanuts, finely chopped
small handful of fresh coriander leaves

TO SERVE
1–2 limes, cut into wedges
sweet chilli sauce

Takes 25–30 minutes • Serves 2–3

1 Put the noodles in a large heatproof bowl, pour boiling water over them and leave for 4 minutes, then drain and refresh under cold running water.
2 Put the lime juice, cayenne, sugar and fish sauce in a bowl and mix well. Have all the other ingredients ready by the cooker.
3 Heat the oil and fry the prawns until warmed through. Add the spring onions and noodles and toss to mix. Tip in the lime juice mixture, then stir in the beansprouts and half the peanuts and coriander. Cook for 1 minute until everything is heated through.
4 Pile into a large dish, scatter with the rest of the peanuts and coriander, and serve with lime wedges and chilli sauce.

• Per serving for two 531 kcalories, protein 27g, carbohydrate 62g, fat 20g, saturated fat 3g, fibre 2g, added sugar 5g, salt 3g

The crab meat should be the freshest available
as this will add extra flavour to the soup.

Crab and Asparagus Soup

175g/6oz white crab meat (fresh or
good-quality canned)
140g/5oz asparagus tips, white or
green
200g/8oz shiitake mushrooms
2 heads pak choi (oriental cabbage)
12 sprigs of fresh coriander
1–2 small fresh red chillies
1.2 litres/2 pints chicken stock
4 tbsp fish sauce
1 tsp coarsely ground black pepper
lime wedges, to serve

Takes about 30 minutes • Serves 6

1 In a small bowl, pick through the crab meat and remove any shell pieces, if using fresh. Rinse and chop the asparagus into small pieces. Remove the stalks from the shiitake mushrooms and slice the caps. Shred and wash the pak choi.

2 Finely shred the coriander and slice the chilli crossways into thin rings, removing the seeds if you don't like your chillies too hot. Set aside.

3 In a large, heavy-based pan, bring the chicken stock to the boil. Add the crab meat, asparagus, mushrooms, pak choi, coriander, fish sauce and black pepper. Return the soup to the boil, stirring. The soup is now cooked.

4 Ladle the soup into bowls and sprinkle with chilli slices. Serve with lime wedges.

• Per serving 51 kcalories, protein 9g, carbohydrate 3g, fat 1g, saturated fat 0g, fibre 0.4g, added sugar 0.2g, salt 3.18g

Even the kids will enjoy the subtle spicing
of this rice dish.

Prawn and Cardamom Rice

50g/2oz butter
1 small onion, finely chopped
1 garlic clove, crushed
10 green cardamom pods, cracked
open
275g/9½oz basmati rice, washed
and drained
small pinch of turmeric
600ml/1 pint hot chicken or
vegetable stock
3 eggs
200g/8oz large cooked peeled
prawns, defrosted and patted
dry if frozen
4 tbsp chopped fresh dill or parsley
200g carton crème fraîche

Takes 30 minutes • Serves 4

1 Preheat the oven to 200°C/Gas 6/fan
oven 180°C. Melt half the butter in a
flameproof casserole dish. Add the onion and
fry until soft. Add the garlic and cardamom
and fry for a minute. Stir in the rice, then the
turmeric and stock. Bring to the boil, cover
and bake for 15–20 minutes. Meanwhile,
place the eggs in a pan of simmering water
for 6 minutes. Drain, then hold under cold
running water to stop cooking.
2 Just before the rice is ready, melt the rest
of the butter in a pan, tip in the prawns and
stir over a low heat for 1 minute or until hot.
Peel and coarsely chop the eggs. Fork the
prawns, eggs and half of the chopped herbs
into the rice. Stir in the crème fraîche and
some seasoning and serve at once,
sprinkled with the remaining herbs.

• Per serving 609 kcalories, protein 25g, carbohydrate
60g, fat 32g, saturated fat 16g, fibre 1g, added sugar
none, salt 1.77g

Trout works a treat with these gentle aromatic flavours.
For a special occasion use snapper or sea bass instead.

Thai Baked Fish

4 trout fillets, about 200g/8oz each
1 lemongrass stalk, finely chopped
small knob of fresh root ginger,
peeled and finely chopped
1 red chilli, seeded and finely
chopped
1 garlic clove, finely chopped
1 tbsp fish sauce
juice of 2 limes
1 tsp golden caster sugar
handful of fresh coriander, roughly
chopped

Takes 20 minutes • Serves 4

1 Preheat the oven to 200°C/Gas 6/fan oven 180°C. Tear off two large sheets of foil and place 1 trout fillet, skin-side down, in the centre of each sheet. Make a sauce by mixing together the remaining ingredients. Spoon half of this mixture over the fillets, setting aside the remainder.

2 Sandwich the other 2 fish fillets on top, skin-side up, then tightly seal the foil to create two packages. Bake for 12–15 minutes. Bring the packages to the table to open and serve with the rest of the sauce.

• Per serving 236 kcalories, protein 40g, carbohydrate 2g, fat 8g, saturated fat 2g, fibre none, added sugar 1g, salt 1.02g

You can cook this classic Chinese dish on the barbecue. Cook for about 1 minute on each side until the flesh is firm and starting to curl.

Salt and Pepper Squid

400g/14oz large squid, or smaller
one totalling the same weight
(the tentacles can be cooked
alongside)
2–3 tbsp olive oil
2 tsp sea salt
½ tsp Chinese five-spice powder
sesame oil, for drizzling
fresh coriander sprigs, to garnish
sweet chilli sauce, to serve

Takes 15–20 minutes • Serves 4

1 Ask the fishmonger to clean the squid; small ones often come ready-cleaned. Using scissors, cut open the body and open out flat. Wash well, then pat dry. If the squid is large, cut the body into 4 roughly square portions.
2 Using the tip of a sharp knife, score the outside of the squid in a criss-cross pattern. Brush with oil and set aside. Mix together the salt, five-spice powder and some pepper. Sprinkle on both sides of the squid just before cooking. You may not need it all.
3 Heat a cast iron ridged griddle pan until hot and cook the squid for about 1 minute on each side, until it starts to curl. Remove with tongs to a serving plate and drizzle with a little sesame oil. Garnish with coriander leaves and serve with small bowls of sweet chilli sauce for dipping.

• Per serving 109 kcalories, protein 16g, carbohydrate 2g, fat 5g, saturated fat 1g, fibre none, added sugar none, salt 1.53g

An eye-catching, prepare-ahead dish
that's brilliant for serving at a party.

Oriental Roast Salmon

1.8kg/4lb salmon, scaled, filleted and
scored, then cut lengthways in half

2 tbsp lime or lemon juice

2 tbsp clear honey

2 tbsp soy sauce

FOR THE STUFFING

large knob of fresh root ginger

1 small fresh red chilli, seeded

1 bunch of spring onions, shredded

2 plump garlic cloves, crushed

2 tbsp sunflower oil

50g/2oz creamed coconut from a
block, chopped or crumbled

400g/14oz raw peeled large prawns

TO GARNISH

1 red chilli, seeded

1–2 spring onions, shredded and
kept in cold water

Takes 1¼ – 1½ hours • Serves 4–6

1 Make the stuffing. Peel the ginger and cut
both it and the chilli into thin strips. Stir fry
the spring onions, chilli, ginger and garlic in the
oil for 3 minutes. Add the coconut and stir
until it melts. Add the prawns and cook until
pink (3 minutes). Season and leave to cool.
2 Preheat the oven to 240°C/Gas 8/fan oven
220°C and put a roasting tray in the oven to
get hot. Sandwich the salmon fillets together
with the stuffing, then tie with string. Lay the
salmon on a sheet or baking parchment, lift
onto the hot tray and roast for 15 minutes.
3 Transfer the salmon to a platter and leave
to rest, covered with foil, for 5 minutes. Heat
the lime juice, honey and soy sauce in a
small pan, pour over the salmon. To garnish,
cut the chilli into very thin strips and sprinkle
over with the spring onions.

• Per serving 736 kcalories, protein 76g, carbohydrate
6g, fat 46g, saturated fat 14g, fibre 2g, added sugar
3g, salt 0.95g

Vietnamese food is simple and fresh-tasting. These rolls are a great combination of tasty crab, crunchy veg, fresh herbs and tangy sauce.

Vietnamese Crab Spring Rolls

2 × 50g packs rice flour pancakes
50g/2oz thin rice noodles
200g can white crabmeat, drained and shredded
1 carrot, finely sliced
½ cucumber, finely sliced
1 red pepper, seeded and finely sliced
Baby Gem lettuce, fresh coriander and mint leaves, to serve

FOR THE DIPPING SAUCE
4 tbsp fish sauce
2 tbsp rice wine vinegar
squeeze of lime
1 red chilli, seeded and finely sliced

Takes 20 minutes • Serves 4

1 Soak the rice flour pancakes according to pack instructions in boiling water for 20 seconds. Remove and cool on kitchen paper. Soak the rice noodles according to pack instructions, drain and cut into 2cm/¾in strips.
2 Lay a rice pancake on a board and arrange some rice noodles, crab, vegetables and herb leaves about a third of the way up, leaving a 1cm/½in edge at the side. Fold the sides over the vegetables and then roll up lengthways to make a cigar. Store in the fridge, covered with moist kitchen paper, for up to 1 day.
3 Mix together the ingredients for the dipping sauce in a bowl. To serve, arrange the rolls on a plate along with the leaves and herbs. To eat, wrap each roll in a piece of lettuce with a herb sprig and dunk into the sauce.

• Per serving 177 kcalories, protein 13g, carbohydrate 31g, fat 1g, saturated fat 0.1g, fibre 1.9g, added sugar 0.3g, salt 3.89g

Index

almonds
    crust with sea bass 106–7
    herby plaice parcels 118–19
anchovy pan bagnat 50–1
asparagus
    and crab soup 200–1
    and prawn puffs 28–9
    and salmon with new potatoes
        128–9
avocado
    and prawn pasta salad 176–7
    and smoked salmon 148–9
    and spinach and prawn salad
        14–15

bagel, smoked salmon and egg
    16–17
basil
    and mustard with herrings 94–5
    and pepper sauce with
        salmon 116–17
beans
    borlotti and prawn salad 24–5
    with pan-fried smoked salmon
        104–5
    salad with griddled tuna 162–3
    and smoked salmon dip 30–1
    tuna-bean toasts 40–1

beetroot
    -cured gravadlax 10–11
    salsa with pan-fried fish 70–1
bouillabaisse, cheat's 96–7
bread, rye with gravadlax and
    cucumber 20–1

cardamom and prawn rice 202–3
ceps and chestnuts with scallops
    100–1
cheese and paprika tuna melts
    26–7
chestnuts and ceps with scallops
    100–1
chickpea and tuna tabbouleh
    174–5
chillies
    chunky seafood stew 178–9
    cream with fishcakes 56–7
cider and garlic sauce with
    mussels 42–3
coconut
    rice, Thai with salmon
        122–2
    spiced with roast salmon
        112–13
cod 62, 96, 114, 136, 156
    herby bake 90–1

with lemon and parsley 82–3
    and zesty roast salmon 142–3
colcannon jackets, smoky 62–3
conversion tables 8–9
crab
    and asparagus soup 200–1
    spicy potted 46–7
    Vietnamese spring rolls
        210–11
cucumber
    with gravadlax and rye 20–1
    relish with tuna steaks 138–9
cullen skink 74–75

dill and smoked salmon tartlets
    38–9
dips 48, 210
    smoked salmon and bean
        30–1

eggs 44, 50
    and smoked salmon bagel
        16–17

fish
    cakes with chilli cream 56–7
    cakes, salmon 180–1
    chunky soup 58–9

finger torpedoes 34–5
grilled with new potato crush 98–9
Mediterranean parcels 158–9
pan-fried with beetroot salsa 70–1
pie, festive 114–15
pie, light and fresh 136–7
pie, superhealthy 156–7
spicy Singaporean 188–9
sweet and spicy 54–5
Thai baked 204–5
Vietnamese fried 196–7

garlic and cider sauce with mussels 42–3
gravadlax
beetroot-cured 10–11
with cucumber and rye 20–1
temptation 130–1

haddock 62, 158
crunchy-topped 110–11
haddock, smoked
cullen skink 74–5
with kale mash 88–9
one-pot 140–1
risotto 150–1
with rocket and rice 154–5
herb noodle and prawn salad 194–5
herbed salmon fillets 78–9
herby almond plaice parcels 118–19
herby cod bake 90–1

herrings 7
with mustard and basil 94–5

Italian-style bass 120–1

kale mash and smoked haddock 88–9
kedgeree, smoked salmon 182–3

leeky salmon in a parcel 66–7
lemon and parsley with cod 82–3
lemongrass with baked sea bass 190–1
lentils and spicy salmon 84–5

mackerel 7
orange-glazed 124–5
peppered and noodles 184–5
mackerel, smoked 160, 182
hot jackets 72–3
salad 170–1
mango green salad with prawns 192–3
Mediterranean fish parcels 158–9
mullet, red, roast with pancetta 126–7
mussels with garlic and cider sauce 42–3
mustard
and basil with herrings 94–5
sauce with poached salmon 108–9

noodles 198, 210
herb noodle and prawn salad 194–5
and peppered mackerel 184–5
nuoc cham sauce 196

one-pot, smoked haddock 140–1
onions
caramelised 108
red and tuna salad 32–3
orange-glazed mackerel 124–5
Oriental roast salmon 208–9

pad Thai 198–9
pancakes 210
pea with smoked salmon 48–9
pancetta with roast red mullet 126–7
paprika 124, 140
tuna and cheese melts 26–7
parsley and lemon with cod 82–3
pasta 22
prawn and avocado salad 176–7
salmon and rocket 92–3
seafood spaghetti 146–7
tuna and pea 168–9
with tuna and tomato 172–3
peas
pancakes with smoked salmon 48–9
and tuna pasta 168–9
pepper and basil sauce with salmon 116–17

pesto 132
   rocket with scallops 22–3
   sauce 64
piperade, prawn 44–5
pizza, ten-minute tuna 164–5
plaice 106
   herby almond parcels 118–19
potatoes
   hot smoked mackerel jackets
     72–3
   kale mash with smoked
     haddock 88–9
   prawn and corn rösti 52–3
   smoky colcannon jackets 62–3
potatoes, new
   crush with grilled fish 98–9
   and hot-smoked salmon salad
     160–1
   with salmon and asparagus
     128–9
   and salmon grill 86–7
   and tuna salad, warm 132–3
   and tuna and spinach salad
     64–5
prawns 114, 156, 182
   and asparagus puffs 28–9
   and avocado pasta salad
     176–7
   bay-scented 36–7
   and borlotti bean salad 24–5
   and cardamom rice 202–3
   and corn rösti 52–3
   and green mango salad 192–3
   and herb noodle salad 194–5
   piperade 44–5

and rice salad 166–7
with romesco sauce 18–19
and spinach and avocado
   salad 14–15

rice
   Mediterranean Tomato 166
   prawn and cardamom 202–3
   and prawn salad 166–7
   and rocket with smoked
     haddock 154–5
   Thai coconut rice with salmon
     122–3
risotto, smoked haddock 150–1
rocket
   pesto with scallops 22–3
   and rice with smoked
     haddock 154–5
   and salmon pasta 98–9
   romesco sauce with prawns
     18–19
rösti, prawn and corn 52–3
rye bread with gravadlax and
   cucumber 20–1

salads
   bean with griddled tuna 162–3
   green mango with prawns
     192–3
   hot-smoked salmon and
     potato 160–1
   potato and tuna, warm 132–3
   prawn and avocado pasta
     176–7
   prawn and borlotti bean 24–5

prawn and herb noodle 194–5
prawn and rice 166–7
smoked mackerel 170–1
smoked trout 144–5
spinach, avocado and prawn
   14–15
tabbouleh with salmon 76–7
tuna, hearty 80–1
tuna, potato and spinach 64–5
tuna and red onion 32–3
salmon 7, 58, 136
   and asparagus with new
     potatoes 128–9
   fishcakes 180–1
   herbed fillets 78–9
   leeky in a parcel 66–7
   lemon-crusted with tzatziki
     102–3
   Oriental roast 208–9
   with pepper and basil sauce
     116–17
   poached with mustard sauce
     108–9
   and potato grill 86–7
   potted fresh and smoked
     12–13
   roast with spiced coconut
     112–13
   and rocket pasta 92–3
   spicy and lentils 84–5
   with tabbouleh salad 76–7
   with Thai coconut rice 122–3
   zesty roast and cod 142–3
salmon, smoked 114 see also
   gravadlax

and avocado 148–9
and bean dip 30–1
and dill tartlets 38–9
and egg bagel 16–17
hot-smoked and potato salad 160–1
kedgeree 182–3
pan-fried with beans 104–5
with pea pancakes 48–9
salsa, beetroot with pan-fried fish 70–1
sardines 7
and watercress on toast 152–3
sauces
adobo 96
chilli 56, 198, 206
fish 192, 196, 198, 200, 204, 210
garlic and cider with mussels 42, 43
horseradish 72, 144
mustard with poached salmon 108–9
nuoc cham 196
pepper and basil with salmon 116–17
pesto 64
romesco with prawns 18, 19
soy 14, 122, 124, 184, 188, 208
scallops
with ceps and chestnuts 100–1
with rocket pesto 22–3
sea bass
with almond crust 106–7

baked with lemongrass 190–1
Italian-style 120–1
seafood
spaghetti 146–7
stew, chunky chilli 178–9
sole 106
goujons 68–9
soup
chunky fish 58–9
crab and asparagus 200–1
cullen skink 74–5
spicy Singaporean fish 188–9
spinach
and avocado and prawn salad 14–15
and tuna and potato salad 64–5
spring rolls, Vietnamese crab 210–11
squid, salt and pepper 206–7
stew, chunky chilli seafood 178–9
sweetcorn and prawn rösti 52–3

tabbouleh
salad with salmon 76–7
tuna and chickpea 174–5
tartlets
prawn and asparagus 28–9
smoked salmon and dill 38–9
Thai baked fish 204–5
Thai coconut rice with salmon 122–3
toasts
sardines and watercress on 152–3

tuna-bean 40–1
tomato
and tuna with pasta 172–3
trout 204
tangy 60–1
trout, smoked 160, 182
salad 144–5
tuna 50, 52, 180, 182
-bean toasts 40–1
and chickpea tabbouleh 174–5
crusty hash 186–7
griddled with bean salad 162–3
paprika and cheese melts 26–7
and pea pasta 168–9
salad, hearty 80–1
and potato salad, warm 132–3
and potato and spinach salad 64–5
and red onion salad 32–3
steaks with cucumber relish 138–9
ten-minute pizza 164–5
and tomato with pasta 172–3
tzatsiki with lemon-crusted salmon 102–3

Vietnamese crab spring rolls 210–11
Vietnamese fried fish 196–7

watercress and sardines on toast 152–3
whiting in a bag 134–5

Picture credits and recipe credits

BBC Worldwide would like to thank the following for providing photographs. While every effort has been made to trace and acknowledge all photographers, we would like to apologize should there be any errors or omissions.

Marie-Louise Avery p47, p69; Iain Bagwell p21, p57, p65, p71, p99, p173, p183; Steve Baxter p141, p165, p205; John Bennett p101; Martin Brigdale p29; Peter Cassidy p11, p119; Jean Cazals p37, p197, p201; Tim Evans-Cook p25; Ken Field p17, p85, p91; Ian Garlick p49; Will Heap p55, p73; Lisa Linder p15; William Lingwood p41, p105, p145; Jason Lowe p185; David Munns p19, p31, p103, p107, p121, p123, p133, p149, p153, p161, p177, p179, p209; Myles New p61; Lis Parsons p211; Michael Paul p113; Juliet Piddington p171; Craig Robertson p43, p79, p95, p97, p125, p127, p135, p155, p189; Howard Shooter p159, p181; Roger Stowell p13, p27, p33, p35, p39, p45, p63, p87, p89, p109, p115, p147, p157, p163, p167, p193, p199, p203; Simon Walton p81, p93, p111, p137, p169, p175, p187; Cameron Watt p117, p139, p207; Philip Webb p23, p77, p83, p151, p191, p195; Simon Wheeler p51, p53, p67, p75, p129, p131, p143; Elizabeth Zeschin p59

The recipes in this book have been created by the editorial team on *BBC Good Food Magazine* and regular contributors to the magazine.